THE BUDGET

TRAVEL GUIDE

THE WORLD IS YOURS

Angelo Omar

The Budget Travel Guide
Copyright © 2024 by Angelo Omar

ISBN: 978-1-958947-29-6

DEDICATION

This book is dedicated to those who have traveled with me physically or through my digital posts and internet presence. Most of all it is dedicated to my mother Irene Hall Dasher for her encouragement to put my travels in a book form. I am thankful for Essie Turner who invited me to apply for a job with Delta Global Services in Atlanta, which allowed me to take many trips around the world. After that job ended I applied for work with Delta Airlines and after getting hired in 2012 I continued my global travels thanks to the flight benefits that Delta offers to its employees. I am so very thankful to God for giving me the health and means to travel and experience so many wonderful adventures.

TABLE OF CONTENTS (1)

Forward
Preface
Introduction

Page

TABLE OF CONTENTS (2)

FOREWORD

Traveling is the dream of many people. Getting to know new places and cultures is a great aspiration and delight. Choosing where to vacation sometimes represents a challenge or an unfavorable choice. The author of this work, Angelo Omar, is a traveler who enjoys getting to know new places and cultures and with this book, he aims to share his experiences with people who love this activity, serving as a reference for key places to visit, communicating prices and incidents along with possible entertainment and recreation activities. His charisma and way of expressing himself, authentic and natural, promote a clear understanding of the message he wants to convey, awakens emotion and interest in enjoying tourism on paradisaical beaches, mountains, cities, amazing places, happy people, delicious food and much more. This work serves as a guide to better take advantage of visits and stays in beautiful places, which provides geographical, economic, climatic and social information about different areas. In this way, people who read this book will have an idea of what to expect, what things they can do and the costs to incur in the different places that the author presents, in the Budget Travel Guide. I invite you to explore this wonderful work and be nourished by its important content, it does not matter if you intend to travel immediately, each narrative is an adventure that you will love to know and live through its stories.

Carmen Yaniras Mendoza, Educator

PREFACE

Traveling the world have indeed been a blessing to me, some my family and also some of my friends. I am thankful to Essie Turner who invited me to apply for a job with Delta Global Services in Atlanta, which allowed me to take many trips since they offered flight benefits. After that job ended I applied for work with Delta Airlines and after getting hired in 2012 I continued my global travels.

I was able to visit many places in the world due to my flight benefits but I still needed to stay within a tight budget because even though I caught the "travel bug", the reality was that I still had a mortgage and other bills to pay regularly.

This book will show you how I traveled to many places on a very limited budget. Keep in mind that my trips took place some years ago and there will be variations to the prices stated in my writings. I hope you enjoy and are able to used some of my tips.

Happy travels and enjoy the book!

INTRODUCTION

Have you ever imagined traveling to far off places and having those "once in a lifetime" moments? Well I have too and fortunately for me I have been able to do it time and time again.

Many people have those same dreams but once they calculate the cost of the trip they puts their dreams on the back burner not realizing that they could actually afford it if they had special tips on how to save money when traveling.

In this book I will attempt to inspire you and show you that you can go to many of the same places that I have traveled to without spending a fortune.

The major costs when traveling are airfare, accommodations, food and tours. I have used Airbnb and Booking.com to arrange most of my accommodations and have done very well with pricing. My per night budget when traveling solo was $40.00 per night in most cases. Keep in mind that many of the trips described in this book were many years ago but I recommend reading many reviews to find rooms, hotels, homes or apartments that are very budget friendly.

For ground transportation I use Uber in many foreign countries which is normally cheaper than the taxis or prearranged transportation. To save on food I try to find accommodations with free breakfast and I eat a lot of fruit. I also cook when I am equipped with a kitchen.

For tours I choose inexpensive or free walking tours which allows you to really soak in the culture of your new environment.

NOTES

CHAPTER ONE - PANAMA

During the first week of November Panama celebrates it's Independence and provided the biggest parade that I have ever witnessed. I couldn't resist the opportunity to see the Panama Canal. Panama City was still in it's rainy season but they were experiencing temperatures in the mid-80's everyday.

We arrived at about 9:00 pm so we relied on the taxi driver to help us locate a reasonably priced hotel. He took us to Hotel Montreal located on Calle Central and was not a bad deal at only $50.00 per night if you book at least two nights. They also have free Wi-fi and a small swimming pool on the roof.

We booked two rooms and stayed there for the two nights then opted to move further down Calle Central to the Euro Hotel where they have Junior Suites with two rooms for only $75.00 per night. They also have free Wi-fi but also offer a free breakfast.

Our first excursion was to the Miraflores Locks of the Panama Canal that was built around 1914.

This is one of the amazing structures that connect the Atlantic and the Pacific Oceans. To get to the Canal you can easily catch a bus to the Al Brook Mall for about 50 cent. The main bus terminal for Panama City is also located at this mall. From there you can catch another bus to the Panama Canal for about $1.00.

When you get off the bus you have about a mile walk to the entrance. You can also catch a taxi from your hotel directly to the entrance which would probably cost about $15.00 - $20.00.

Once inside you can enjoy a historical video presentation that describes the tedious work that was required to build the Panama Canal locks. You can also go out and witness the locks in action. Steven Tyler of the American Idol series happened to be getting a special tour during the same time we made our visit. At night the Casino and Club section located on Calle Uruguay comes alive but on the actual first day of the Independence celebration everything shuts down.

It is the memorial commemoration and no alcohol is sold and no clubs are open for that 24 hour period. Schools are also closed.

Photo by A. Omar Muhammad (c) 2011

The stores are open and many people visit the area called Cinco de Mayo which is one of the main shopping areas in the downtown section.

Anticipation for the parade following the memorial day is high and we met some people who have been coming to Panama for over ten years to enjoy the festivities. The parade starts about 10:00 am and was still going strong when we left at 3:00 pm just when the daily rain began to fall. I was told that the parade used to run from 10:00 am to 10:00 pm.

The uniforms, the colors, the children, and the tremendous crowd all add to the flavor of the day. Great bands and dancers along with motorcycles and jeeps add to the energy and sounds of the parade.

Photo by A. Omar Muhammad (c) 2011

We also attempted to go to the ruins in Portebelo but it did not work out because we did not get an early start. Set aside a full day and start out early if you want to include this in your itinerary. Portebelo is a small town on the coast which has the remains of Spanish forts and it is a UNESCO World Heritage Site. We tried to do it in a half day and it's just not enough time. Once again you must take a bus to the Al Brook Mall and switch to the bus to Colon. About 15 minutes before you reach Colon you get off the bus and take the bus to Portebelo.

Photo by A. Omar Muhammad (c) 2011

We pushed forward into the city of Colon but again it was late in the day and not much going on. Many stores were closed in the run down business area so once we got to the bus terminal in Colon we just boarded another bus headed back to the Al Brook mall. I'm sure that Colon has some nice things to offer if we had more time to explore that area. Another hour and a half ride was ahead of us heading back, but Colon did not appear to have much to offer at that time of the evening and we were advised by some locals that were riding the bus with us the Colon may not be a safe place to be at night for tourists.

-

Photo by A. Omar Muhammad (c) 2011

Once we made it back to the mall we went to Nikos Restaurant for some delicious food. Nikos is a chain restaurant with various locations around Panama. Offering a variety of dishes at very reasonable prices makes this a great choice for a sit down meal. I enjoyed fish, squash, and chicken soup. They also offer a variety of fresh juices including mango, papaya, pineapple and others.

-

b

At night, one of the casinos came alive with a live band performing and other bands performed in other areas around the city all in celebration of independence week.

In anticipation of an early flight back to Atlanta, GA, I knew that I would be missing out on many other festivities being offered in Panama. It's a great place to be, even in their rainy season because of Independence week but according to the locals, it would also be a great place to be during the Christmas season or in February during the Carnival.

With that in mind, I'll keep Panama on my list as a future travel option.

Travel Safe Everyone!

CHAPTER TWO

NICARAGUA

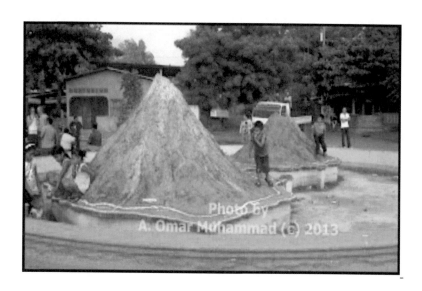

Photo by A. Omar Musa Kmad (c) 2013

e

My trip to Nicaragua really got a jump-start as soon as I boarded
the plane and was greeted by Frank, a world traveler and
knowledgeable businessman, who had a lively spirit and generated
much energy among the passengers seated in the front row of first
class. He also kept Mila, the flight attendant, on her toes. The
flight from Atlanta to Managua, Nicaragua was about four hours
and gave Frank time to provide me with some very helpful tips in
navigating my way around Nicaragua. He lives in Connecticut but
has a home in Costa Rica and in Astillero, Nicaragua. He also talked
about purchasing full containers of products from China and selling
the items for profits but emphasized the importance of having the
items already pre-sold before placing the order. He invited me to
come and visit him at his "small" place and his traveling partner
Donald agreed that it was a good idea.

The deplaning process in Managua was quick and going through customs was a breeze. It only took about fifteen minutes to get checked in at customs. There are only about four baggage carousels which are located to the right after exiting the customs area. The tourism information desk is before you get to the baggage area.

This is run by the Board of Tourism and the young man actually shut down his station to make sure he directed me to a good taxi driver. He said the Board of Tourism wants to make sure that tourist have a good experience so would come back again. The taxi fare was $10.00 for the 20 minute ride to Hostel Nicaragua.

I booked this guest house on booking.com for $16.00 per night which included free breakfast, wifi, and cable tv. By the time I settled in, it was after 10:00 pm, just in time for the Floyd Mayweather fight. I used the microwave in the lobby to pop some corn and sat there with the receptionist and watched the fight being aired on the En Vivo channel.

In the morning I took a cool shower, which was fine after night in the very modest and non-air-conditioned room. I did enjoy the fresh fruit they provided for breakfast. I was now ready for my trip to the beach at San Juan Del Sur.

The hostel owners were very nice and even walked me to the main road to catch the local bus to the central bus station. From there I would board the express bus to Rivas. From there I would take the final bus to San Juan Del Sur. The total time of the trip on the three buses will take about three hours but will cost less than $10.00 to get there. The bus is the best way to see the country and experience the culture of the people.

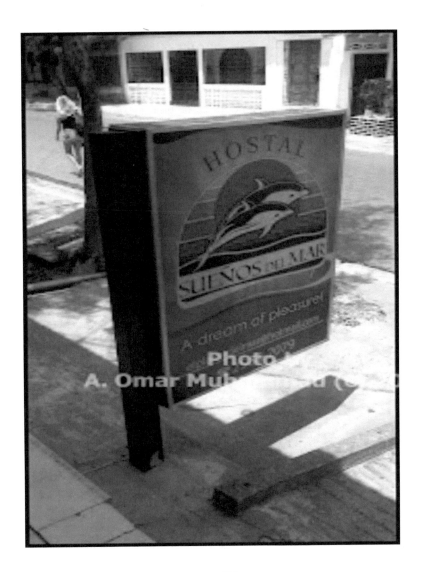

Once I arrived in San Juan Del Sur, it took a while to find the Suenos Del Sur Hostel which I also booked using booking.com but the name was listed as Sueflos and I walked past the place and around the block, asking many people, before I found it. This hostel had private rooms along with dorms for about $9.00 per night. I upgraded to a private room which cost $20.00 (this is equal to about 500 cordobas). They had free wifi but no breakfast. It is also located about three blocks from the beach. There were numerous other options right on the beach.

Photo by
A. Omar Muhammad (c) 2013

I spent most of the day on the beach and taking some intermittent dips in the water. I had chicken salad for lunch at Restaurante El Timon which is a nice beachfront eatery. I had a nice peaceful day but began to feel that one day in this "touristy" area was enough for me to get the flavor of this place, so I had a very nice dinner at the Café Mediteranneo Restaurant that night prepared by Chef Giovanni, consisting of fish sautéed in wine sauce, rice and greens.

I got up early the next morning and went jogging and then on to the best yoga class ever, headed by Mali, who was filling in for someone else.

Afterwards I got a smoothie, went back to the hostel to take a quick shower and checked out.

I took a taxi to Rivas for $5.00 which is about 20 miles away. The next bus wasn't scheduled to leave until 2:30pm and my plan was to make it to Ometepe Island where there are two non-active volcanoes. I stopped at a bakery and got a pound cake topped with pineapple. I walked around Rivas checking out some of the stores but all I bought was some fresh tomatoes. I then jumped into a crowded taxi and headed for San Jorge which is where you can go to the pier and catch the ferry over to Ometepe. The hour long ferry ride costs only $2.00 or 50 cordobas. The return trip back to the mainland will cost you a bit more.

I got off the ferry with no idea where I was going or even where I was going to stay that night, so I took the low bidder who was willing to take me closer to one of the volcanoes even though I had no plans to climb it. If you enjoy climbing then your best option would be to position yourself in a hotel or hostel so you could get an early start on your climb the following morning. If you are like me and only want exterior pictures, then you can stay in a place near the ferry or make the trip to next day. The area near the ferry is much busier with shops, restaurants and hostels than the areas like Santo Domingo and Conception, that are about 45 minutes away, which are urged on by taxi drivers trying to make more money. They will tell you that the best places are one hour away and will try charging you $40.00 or more. The price quickly declines as more drivers surround you bidding on your business. You can get one of them to drive you for about $12.00.

I was driven by Oscar, a bit older than the majority of the other drivers and less anxious. Once we arrived in Santo Domingo I decided on Hotel Azul. I think I was the only guest in the entire hotel. It was a very nice place on the beach but probably due to inactivity, the upkeep was not the best and there were knats flying around everywhere.

I paid about $15.00 for the room facing the beach. It was a family operation and the owners were very nice. Francisco Quinta, one of the brothers, lives in Chicago but was on vacation. He is an international chef but I did not get a chance to sample his food because I arrived so late. He spoke very good English and showed me around after I had settled in. We went to the Hotel Villa Paraiso, just down the road so I could have dinner and then over to Conception to relax at a place called Rancho Sabor Isleno.

The next morning I got up early about 6am a took a quick cold shower and made my way down to the dining area to find Francisco already up, finishing his breakfast and ready to go.

He took me across the street to meet his 99 year old mom and other members of his family. His father joined us as we headed to the volcano to get a closer look. We circled the entire volcano which was a grueling, bumpy and tedious trip. I would not suggest riding around the volcano because the road is not fit to be traveled on and it takes more than 2 hours to make it around.

The best option is to go to the right when you approach the circle of the Santo Domingo side. Drive in about 10 to 15 minutes and then turn around. By that time you will likely see monkeys and some of the modern homes that have been built there. We finished up with revolution around the volcano about 10:45 am and Francisco took me back to the ferry. He was very kind and did not even accept a tip or payment for extending himself the way he did. I had some time to grab a bite to eat and decided to have pizza at Pizzaria Buon Appetito, located in Moyogalpa, near the entry area for the ferry. The pizza was great and is highly recommended.

I arrived back in San Jorge and grabbed a taxi to Rivas for 30 cordobas. My next move was to find another taxi to Tola and then on to Astillero to see Frank, who I mentioned earlier, who had extended an invitation to me on the plane.

I spoke to someone about my plans to go and they said if you get an invitation in Nicaragua, you should try to fulfill it if you feel right about it. That's why I made the journey to see Frank, because it felt right. My taxi from Rivas to Astillero was $40.00 USD or 1,000 cordobas

Photo by A Omar Muhammad (c) 2013

The only thing I had was a note that Frank wrote with his address. I remembered when I asked Frank how I would find him, he said, "just ask around for Franko, everybody knows me". One person we asked for directions sent us the wrong way to a huge house. We pulled up to the gate and one of the workers said we were at the wrong house. He said to go further up the hill to another "casa" which he described as "grande". Now if the guy in this huge house is calling another house "grande" then you have to start to wonder. We went up the road a bit more and there it was.. Casa Con Domo Azul.

The gate keepers checked things out and let us through. The house is a short drive or a good walk from the road. I was a bit shocked at the beauty of the house.

We knocked on the huge doors, surrounded by blue tiled beams, which match the many domes on the house. As we were escorted through the enormous foyer containing a Greek god statue, super high ceiling and spiral marble staircases I noticed that my driver Javier was almost as excited as me. We walked through the professional styled kitchen and walked out the patio doors exposing me to a fabulous built in pool that has a continuous running vision as if the water continues into the Pacific Ocean.

Photo by
A. Omar Muhammad (c) 2013

I said "Franko, I was looking for this little place that you told me about". Frank looked up from the center of the pool, with his relaxed cool attitude, and said "what do you think?". Frank also asked me what was the one word that would describe what I thought when I walked in.

Photo by
A. Omar Muhammad (c) 2013

I responded saying it was either "Kingdom" or "Paradise". Looking at this magnificent mansion on the beach you would think that Frank was born into a wealthy family but this is not the case. He still remembers standing in lines with his mother to get bread, soup and a block of cheese after his father left Italy, and headed to America in search of a better life. His father became a barber and saved enough to buy a three family house. He promised Frank that he would put him through college and law school. Frank eventually did finish college and wanted to attend law school in England but got rejected. He had a talk with God and promised God that if He got him in the school, that he would build Him a church one day.

He got into the law school and opened his practice in Meredith, CT. Frank and his partners also began to make real estate deals and owned a large portfolio of properties. During a large city gathering concerning construction projects, a church building committee approached him and asked if he could build their church. When Frank looked at the plans he told them that it would cost in excess of $25 million to build it and told them they did not have that kind of money.

The church committee said they could come up with the funding but got turned down for their loan. In the meantime, Frank had a dream about the promise that he made to God about building Him the church and decided he would build the church with his own money. The AME church stands today in Middletown, CT.

Frank has continued his charitable giving in Nicaragua and was also building a school and orphanage near his home.

I have personally witnessed his generosity, not only by his invitation to me to stay at his fabulous home for two days, but also the way he hosted Bishop Jorge Solarsano along with some nuns from the Granada Cathedral, and a delegation of pastors from Tola, not only providing food and drinks but also cooking all of the food himself. After my two days of relaxing in this luxurious home it was time to move on to my next destination.

After Frank paid his cleaning and grounds keeping staff he and
Donald were heading back to Managua and said he would drop me
off in the historic city of Granada. He stopped in Rivas to get a
haircut and treated us to a wonderful meal at Mi Pueblo
Restaurant which is an unassuming but growing restaurant located
in Belin, just outside of Rivas. I ate the best succulent grilled
chicken I ever tasted.

He ordered the Plato Especiale which feeds about five people and includes various meats, plantains, nachos, plantain chips and bean dip. Be sure to specify whether or not you want pork included.

Photo by A. Omar Muhammad (c) 2013

Once I arrived in Granada, I stopped into an internet cafe to find a reasonable hotel. I found the Granada Spa Hotel, which had large rooms, a nice pool, free wifi and a fantastic free breakfast. I paid $57.00 which is more than my normal hotel budget but the hotel was in a good location and it was nice.

After checking in I walked over to Bienvenido a la Torre de la Merced which is a tower attached to a church where you can pay $1.00 and walk up the stairs and get a beautiful view of Granada. I walked over to a café to have a small bite to eat. I didn't need much because the lunch was so filling. I decided to have an avocado salad and it was a good choice.

There were many other people sitting outside having dinner and drinks and watching some of the entertainers who move from one area to another performing for tips. There are also many vendors who will approach you selling hammocks, bracelets and other items. There are also a few street walkers who stroll up and down near the restaurants asking men if they want company. The next morning I got up early and went around to take some more photos in this historic town including shots of the oldest building in Central America which is a church that has now been converted to a museum. I checked out of the hotel and walked around doing some shopping and then headed for the bus station. It was now Friday and I had been in Nicaragua since Saturday.

I took the bus into Managua and decided that I would only stay one more night and head to the airport in the morning for a return flight to Atlanta.

d

The King's Palace and decided to get off the bus and check it out. I negotiated a rate of $35.00 and settled in to the modest room. The A/C did not work that well but they did have free wifi and was located across from the Pharaoh Casino and restaurants like Fridays. I flagged down a taxi and he dropped me off near a large modern mall where there were many stores including Payless Shoes. It was a lively atmosphere with music and dancers dressed in colorful outfits. I got some yogurt at TCBY and sat down to relax and listen to the cultural music. On the other end of the bench was a woman and her young son, who looked at me with playful curiosity. He gently broke free of his mothers grip and scurried down my end of the bench and jumped in my arms and just melted. He laid there on my chest as if he knew I cared for him and I did. His mother smiled with both embarrassment and admiration. The child slowly raised up off my chest and returned to his mother. He was playing with a bag filled with his clean diapers, throwing it up in the air. At that moment I knew my next move. I was going to find a toy store and buy my new friend a ball to play with. I asked his mother what his name was and she said it was Hombre'. When I returned with the ball I reached out to give it to him and looked surprised as if to say "really! for me". Spending those few minutes with Hombre' was the best feeling I had that day. I left the mall and went to the casino, lost $20.00 at the blackjack table then headed to Fridays for some food. I was tired and took the food back to the hotel to eat while I watched the NBA playoff game. I couldn't get through the second game without falling asleep. I had a 7:25 am flight and got up the next morning at 4:45am, took a quick shower and ran out to meet me prearranged taxi at 5:00am. Managua airport here I come.

I used the last of my cordobas on souvenirs and headed through the security checkpoint.

I guess I would have to see Leon and the Corn Islands another time. I looked forward to returning to Nicaragua the following year with twelve to sixteen youth who would gain much inspiration and education by visiting this diverse, cultural, scenic and historic place. Unfortunately, the youth trip never materialized due to a lack of funding through our non-profit organization Giving Initiatives and Alternatives, Inc.

It's very affordable to travel throughout the country and provides great opportunity to learn and be inspired by this rich culture.

CHAPTER THREE

Paradise Found in Negril, Jamaica

I started my year off with a bang by heading to Jamaica on January 1st. This turned out to be a great time to go, not just because they have 85 to 90 degree weather but also because many states throughout the US experience bone chilling temperatures during that time even in Atlanta, GA.

After arriving in Montego Bay from Atlanta on a flight that only took about three hours, I made arrangements with Juta Tours to transport me to Negril which is on the west side of the island and about 90 minutes away.

Juta Tours has a reception desk located to the left as you exit the customs area. Nicole was very attentive and helpful and the driver was very professional. You can also arrange transportation in advance.

Once in Negril, I found a place to stay across the street from the beachfront resorts which was much cheaper. I paid $30.00 per night for a clean secure room with a shower, hot water and a small refrigerator. The owner, Cecil Tate (known as Baully), lives in the front house with his granddaughter Shai and her son. Mr. Tate had five rental units and four of them also included a small stove at a slightly higher rate.

He has since suffered a fire in some of his units but is located diagonally across from the Negril Tree House Resort where my friend Julius was staying with his family.

They along with a large group of others have made the an annual trip, some have been coming for the last 20 years and always stay at the Negril Tree House which is a very nice resort with air conditioned rooms ranging from $135 to $250 per night. The owner, Gail Jackson is very friendly and you will normally see her moving around greeting guests and welcoming new arrivals. She even made me feel welcome knowing that I was a friend of Julius even though I wasn't staying there. Chantell, Karen, and the other staff also made me feel at ease about my numerous daily visits. The website is Negril-treehouse.com.

I went swimming and then had a bite to eat right there at the Tree . I had a fish burger, rice and beans and some lettuce and tomato which costs about $11.00.

The next day (Thursday) I got up and went for a 20 minute jog on the main road. It was the perfect preparation for a yoga class at the Negril Tree House given by Jessica Johnson who was giving regular classes there. It was a great, calm routine with low to moderate difficulty. She is from Pittsburgh, PA but had been living in Jamaica for three years now.

Jessica and her husband Nigel also manufacture almond oil. I ate at Sheritas which is situated right on the beach about a three minute walk from the Tree House. I enjoyed a great view as I ate another fish burger with rice and beans for about $9.00. It was a standard meal but the waiter, also named Omar, was very nice. I met some of the others who had come to Jamaica with Julius' group and had great laughs with Lori from Connecticut before turning in.

My third day in Negril I got up early to take in the nature of my surroundings and decided to take a stroll in the backyard area. I saw a big tree and thought I could use it to do some pull-ups but when I jumped up and grabbed the branch, it cracked open sounding like it had been struck by lightening. The large branch came tumbling down as I struggled to hold it, and the attached clothes line, steady. Well, the clothes that were on the line never hit the ground and I leaned the branch against the tree trunk.

I waited for Baully to come out his back door so I could break the news to him personally. I offered to cut up the branch and carry to the back but he said don't worry about it.

I went over and had the buffet breakfast at the Negril Tree House, complete with a waffle, callaloo, fish, fruit, banana bread, oatmeal and raisin bread. It was $13.00 and I got my moneys worth. Afterwards I went swimming and since it was Friday, when I saw a young Muslim couple I asked them if they knew where the Masjid was. Taghreed and her husband Sammy were a beautiful young couple who had roots in Syria and now live in Orlando, Florida. They, like me wanted to attend Jumuah prayer. After getting sketchy instructions, Julius, myself and the couple went out to prayer.

 We had a great time with all the Muslims and after prayer, they served us a spicy rice dish with curry goat. Afterwards we stopped at Ricks Café, which is a very popular tourist stop, and watched some of the brave travelers and locals jump off the cliff into the water about 80 feet below. Later that evening Taghreed, Sammy and myself went to the Sweet Spice Restaurant for dinner. This restaurant has been around for many years and is now a favorite among locals and visitors. The portions seemed to be getting a bit smaller compared to my visit there thirteen years ago. It is located on White Hall Road and is about a ten minute ride from the beach strip area. We had desert at the OMG Ice Cream store which is also on White Hall Road. I had the carrot cake while Taghreed and Sammy had ice cream.

When we got back to the Negril Tree House, we watched some of the guests who were lighting some floating lamps that were released into the sky.

I left the next morning with Monica and Nadia at 8:45am headed to Kingston. I really felt the need to see the Bob Marley Museum so I jumped at the opportunity to go. The museum is located at 56 Hope Road, Kingston 6, and the telephone number is (876) 927-9152. I highly recommend the tour. Monica, who had rented a car, is a real trooper on the road and drove the whole way.

During the tour we noticed Bob Marley's son Damian was on the premises so we went outside to greet him and take photos. He was very approachable and easy going. He was having his annual benefit concert that night along with Shaggy with the majority of proceeds going to help children. As we returned to the tour I felt great knowing that Bob Marley lived in the house that I was walking through.

We went to the New Kingston Business Centre to pick up a few things before going to eat at the So So Restaurant located at 4 Chelsea Ave, KGN 10. I had the best meal of the trip up to that point which consisted of a whole steamed red snapper fish with coconut sauce and okra.

IT WAS DELICIOUS! It did take a long time to prepare but the $14.00 meal was worth it. They can be reached at (876) 968-2397. We had found the restaurant by asking a local driver where he ate and he provided a few names of places before suggesting that he take us over to SoSo.

We arrived back in Negril around 12:30 am after a long, long day on the road.

The next day (Sunday) was pretty relaxing. I started the day with some fruit and then decided to go for a light jog on the beach. I also did some pull-ups on a tree that extends out to the shoreline (this time the branch did not break).

Afterwards I walked and met some of the vendors, including Mason, who is one of the chief sculpture a artists and is located at the craft center near Alfreds. I also talked to Jwajiku, who was also a part of the large group with Julius. She is a retired teacher and author who spends 3 to 4 months a year in Negril.

For lunch I only had one cucumber that I bought along the beach so I was ready for a good meal at dinner time. I went to the Best of the West Jerk and got a half chicken with rice and beans and cabbage and it was plenty. They provide the jerk sauce on the side so you can use the amount that best suits you.

They are very friendly and the portions are great. After the meal, Julius and I walked across the street to the Sun Beach Restaurant and Bar to hear some live performances. The band and artists were good, including two of the female artists named Queen Makada and Queen Abiona. I also met one of the owners of the Sunbeach named Andrea who was very pleasant and welcoming. They also rent rooms.

Monday was uneventful during the day except for a trip downtown to the grocery store. Julius and I detoured into a neighborhood that I had visited back in 2000 when I first went to Negril. With the help of some youngsters that Julius knew when they were babies, I found Simon who sells barbeque elements, nitro gas logs and fencing.

He lives just down the road from the Sweet Spice Restaurant and can be reached at (876) 368-0806. Simon also grows plantain and has a large apple tree on his land. It was good seeing him after so many years. That evening we went to Roots Bamboo for more live music from Queen Abiona and Charlie Chaplan.

Tuesday arrives and I wanted to relax a bit so I got up and ate some fruit and cereal that I bought at the market. I went over to the beach to swim and all was going well until Julius and Juelle decided to finally go jet skiing after a week of talking about it. I volunteered to videotape them and forgot that my telephone was in my pocket as I walked out into the ocean. That was a real bummer!

Julius and the large group with him were leaving so I greeted many of them as they boarded their bus headed to the airport. I was also supposed to leave but the standby list did not show any seats available. For dinner I went back to the Best of the West, this time only ordering a quarter chicken.

On Wednesday, I went to Mayfield Falls with Jannie who came from California and her friend. It was really a stream of large rocks mixed with small areas to swim. It was beautiful and peaceful as you are slowly guided through by the tour guide.

There is a $15.00 entry fee and the tour guide also will request a tip. We also paid $30.00 each to Butter, who was our driver. He is dependable and normally positioned at the entry area of the Negril Tree House.

We opted out of the optional lunch which is also an additional fee. A photographer also shoots many pictures and you can purchase a disk at the end of your tour for about $40.00. I would not highly recommend this tour because of the many fees and because it is more of a rolling stream as opposed to a waterfall. I took a nap when we returned to prepare for the big Luciano Show that evening. Luciano is a well known reggae artist who has traveled to world and he did not disappoint. He put on a fabulous show that I will remember for many years to come. He sang a variety of songs with many giving praise to the most high creator. He also sang songs in honor of women. His deep reggae soul sound should not be missed and with ticket prices at only $15.00 this was the biggest bargain in Negril.

I got up Thursday and went with Jwajiku to Abiona's Juice Bar, located on the west end just in front of the Islamic Center, to taste her okra juice. and her sorrel punch . They were both very good. Abiona also cooks light meals made to order. Afterwards we headed to the market to buy some groceries. Tasha, one of my neighbors, who works as a chef at Hotel Real, said she would cook food for me if I bought it. She cooked rice and peas, vegetables and chicken. The plate was professionally laid out and everything was amazingly delicious! The food was so good you could taste it before you put it in your mouth! She credits her mother with teaching her how to cook. The next night was equally delicious replacing the chicken with basa fish and plantain. Her meals were the best and even better than the coconut fish I had at the So So Restaurant in Kingston, which was hard to beat.

After eating I relaxed and headed out to Bourbon Beach for a free reggae show. Like most shows, it did not start until just before midnight. I was invited by Queen Makada but she did not perform that night. I did get a chance to buy some her products from her vending space that she occupies daily at the Bourbon Beach. Her products include bracelets, clothing and other souvenirs.

Friday was my last full day in Jamaica so I wanted it to be easy going. I started by connecting with Sandy, who I met at the Luciano show and said she could take me to Silver Springs, which is a small untapped natural spring of circulating water that is still used by the locals to drink and bathe. As we sat there, a few people came to wash and some came to collect water. It was amazing to see and I even got a chance to wet my feet in this water that seemed magical.

Saturday I got up early, took a shower and headed to the airport. Along the way I stopped in Orange Bay to see a small community where people still live in one room shacks but paradise surrounds them. Many don't have televisions or radios and it is not an issue. As I walked along the coastline greeting the people, a feeling of serenity was all around me.

I headed to the airport with a feeling in my gut like a child who was about to leave his grandmothers house. My flight was delayed for two hours which gave me time to go downtown Montego Bay and soak up another hour of sunshine. JAMAICA!! If you haven't been, you better go so you too can experience PARADISE!! Jah Rastafari. Yah Mon!!!

CHAPTER FOUR

Cruise to the Bahamas for Affordable Fun

We booked a five day, four night Carnival Cruise leaving out of Jacksonville, FL in October and it only cost about $1,000.00 for four people. Since I live near Atlanta GA, I have the option of either driving about six hours or taking a 45 minute flight to Jacksonville. I opted to fly, of course, since my family and I enjoy the flying benefits that we have courtesy of Delta Airlines.

Photo by
A. Omar Muhammad (c) 2012

We arrived at the Jacksonville airport at 11:30am and was at the port by about 12:30pm.

Taxi service will cost between $30.00 and $35.00 dollars each way. The boarding process is a bit long with many other passengers also waiting in the general boarding or V.I.P. line. Our departure time was 4:00 pm and Carnival requires that you arrive two hours prior to departure.

Once we finished processing our document s at check in and received our cabin keys we rushed off to drop our bags in the room, then off to the buffet we went. There are 24 hour food stations available, offering pizza, burgers and fries in addition to the breakfast, lunch and dinner buffet selections that are available daily. Breakfast choices include eggs, pancakes, fresh fruit, hot or cold cereal, grits, sausage and more. Lunch sometimes includes chicken nuggets, fries, rice and beans, jerk chicken, plaintain, backed fish, stir fry vegetables and more. You can also choose to sit and eat in the formal dining areas for breakfast, lunch and dinner where there are often different selections.

There is a spa and gym onboard for those who want to keep up with their exercise routines. Additional fees apply for most of the spa activities but the gym is free.

Photo by
A. Omar Muhammad (c) 2012

There are many other activities on board including art auctions, shopping specials, dance classes, ice carving and towel folding demonstrations, and many trivia games that sometimes offer prizes to the participants and winners. The casino is open most of the time and there are nightly shows in the theaters, clubs and in other meeting rooms. My favorites are the comedy and the themed dance shows. The family comedy shows are the earlier shows and the adult comedy shows are later in the evening. The service on this particular Carnival Cruise was fairly good overall but there are incidents that makes it appear as though Carnivals service standards are slipping. Some of the other guests that I spoke to also noticed the same lack of service, ironically in the formal dining rooms, where you might expect the best service.

Photo by
A. Omar Muhammad (c) 2012

Carnival also offers a free drink to the VIP and return travelers, but the drinks are only available during certain times and in one location on the ship, so even though many guests would like to take advantage of the free drink coupon, they either can't find the location or they are involved with other activities on the ship.

First time cruisers should keep in mind that Carnival Cruise Lines will automatically deduct the gratuities from your credit card on file for each person traveling with you (even children). So, if you have a family of four, you would be charged an additional $184.00 to cover tips. To avoid this, always go to guest services and inform them that you will pay your own gratuities in cash and that the deductions should not be charged on your credit card. You can then, pay out your tips to the individuals that are providing you with excellent service.

We made stops at Freeport and Nassau during the cruise, which gives passengers the opportunity to get off the boat for the day and explore the islands, go on tours, shop or go to the beach. This is a great way to break up your trip and get on some land in between.   Once you get to the beach you can go jet skiing or ride a banana boat. Just be sure and get back to the ship an hour before sailing time.

Photo by
A. Omar Muhammad (c) 2012

This cruise was a very affordable way to take a family vacation in a safe environment. Children even have the option of going to camps that are divided up based on their ages but be mindful that for children over 11 years of age, there is not much supervision involved and some of the youth activities extend late into the night. Where else can you go on vacation and only pay about $50.00 dollars a day per person, have a place to sleep and eat all of the food you could stuff into your body? Even with their few service shortcomings and their sometimes all too obvious focus on the bottom line, Carnival stays on my list as a recommended choice when seeking entertaining budget travel.

CHAPTER FIVE

Boca Chica and Santo Domingo Dominican Republic

I wanted to go on a quick getaway for just a couple of days where the weather was nice enough to spend some time on the beach but in October the choices are narrowed due to many of the Caribbean islands are hit with rainfall during this time of the year.

My search led me to Boca Chica and Santo Domingo in the Dominican Republic where the forecasts were showing 80-85 degree weather with only a 20-30% chance of rain. The flight is only about four hours from Atlanta, GA so off I went.

The Las Americas International Airport in the Santo Domingo area is pleasant and unassuming especially in low season.

It was much more congested on my previous visit there in January of 2010, when I passed through the airport enroute to Haiti after they had suffered from the devastating earthquake. The taxi services are readily available once you pass through customs and collect your baggage. The ride to Santo Domingo cost about $30.00 and to Boca Chica is about $20.00. It is cheaper if you take Uber.

The first night there I stayed at the Don Juan Resort in Boca Chica which is an all-inclusive resort that left many things to be desired. The water did not really get hot in the sink or shower. The restaurants and grill did not have anything for me to eat except pizza. The main restaurant that offered breakfast, lunch and dinner opened on time but the buffet items while offering fish, chicken, and various salads did not hit the mark as far as taste is concerned. Even the fish soup was probably the worst that I had ever had.

The food was certainly edible and since I had paid $120.00 to stay there, that was even more of an incentive to eat to try and get my moneys worth.

The layout of the food was great and the waiters and waitresses performed their duties with precision. The pool was nice which I enjoyed but the gym was small and filled with mosquito's, which cut my workout short. The view from the balcony in my room overlooking the beach was beautiful. I was on the third floor and the four story hotel did not have elevators.

The tour office was closed during some of the advertised hours of normal operation so I waited until the following day to book a tour. My plan was to take a half day tour that would allow me to see some sights and then get dropped off at the Palacio Hotel in Santo Domingo where I had booked a room for my second nights stay. Needless to say, I was happy to have checked out of the Don Juan Resort after arranging the tour for only $35.00. A taxi would have cost about the same price or more to just take me to the Palacio.

Many tours will allow you to be picked up at one location and be dropped off at another. You should ask before you book your tour.

The tour started off at Volvamos Al Verde which is an underground cave and stream. It is a beautiful sight to see that looked like a scene from a James Bond movie. I would highly recommend a visit to this cave if you go to the Santo Domingo area. We also visited many statues of Christopher Columbus who is known as Cristobal Colon by many Dominicans. We visited an old church and a fort still equipped with old canons facing the water.

The tour guide could only speak a little English and had it not been for another person on the tour who spoke Spanish and English I would have been much less informed. Always request a tour guide that speaks your language when booking a tour.

The Palacio Hotel sits right in the Colonial District and there is easy walking access to many stores, gift shops and street vendors in the area. The hotel is pleasing to the eye from the lobby to the rooms and even boasts marble bathrooms. They also have a small rooftop pool, free breakfast and free internet access. I would recommend this hotel to others, but don't leave your bags on the floor. My only complaint was seeing a trail of ants that had invaded my suitcase that I left on the floor. After checking in I went out to check out the local sites and buy a few souvenirs. The main strip was lively with music, vendors and plenty of girls trying to make a profitable "love" connection. The Dominican Republic remains one of my most visited countries.

CHAPTER SIX

Belize

I needed a break from the regular hustle and bustle of everyday living and working and shopped around for a for a place to go for a few days. I always prefer 80 degree or above temperatures in my vacation destination.

So I continued with my search for a suitable location to travel to and found that Belize was experiencing beautiful weather ranging from 78 to 82 degrees during the time I would be traveling. The choice was easy and I was on my way.

I arrived at the Belize airport and needed to get to one of the hotels that I had researched on the Frommers website. I always try to get some background data about the places I plan to travel to and for some reason I trust the information I get from the Frommers site.

The taxi ride from the airport in to the city area of Belize cost $25.00 US dollars or BZ$50. The Belcove Hotel where I checked in cost $34.00 US and is situated in the heart of the Belize City. The hotel is very quaint but was adequate for my needs except for not having internet service. The room had a TV, with many sports channels, a shower, a fan and a nice balcony that overlooked the bridge that carried cars and pedestrians back and forth constantly throughout the day.

I was a bit tired and did not do much that day except get a mediocre meal next door to the hotel and relax on the balcony. At night I took a taxi over to the Princess Hotel, which is a larger hotel whose amenities include a bowling alley, an arcade and a casino.

I was able to check my email there for BZ$5.00 per half hour of use.

I went back to the Belcove to relax because I planned to catch the first boat heading to Ambergris Caye in the morning. Ambergris is a separate island. The water taxis are walking distance from the Belcove and the price to ride is BZ$55.00 or about $27.50 US round trip. The ride takes about an hour an a half.

I checked into Ruby's which is another very quaint place, but this one happens to be right on the beach, has free internet service and only cost $27.50 US or BZ$55.00. Like the Belcove these accommodations are for people who require the minimum room amenities and are not for guests seeking luxurious surroundings. This room did not have a television but had a fan and a private shower.

I arranged a tour with the hotel receptionist and she connected me with a young man named Dennis, who did an excellent job taking me to many areas in his golf cart, which is the main mode of transportation.

One of the highlight of his tour was a visit to a Butterfly farm and to the small airport named The Tropic, which runs flights back and forth from Belize International.

I ate at a restaurant on South Street and tried the Fish Ceriviche, which was praised by some of the Belizeans but did not impress me.

I went for a walk in the evening to replenish my water supply a got a great treat when I walked past a sports bar and heard on the outside speaker "The Executioner". I turned back, went inside and to my surprise, Bernard Hopkins was about to fight. Needless to say, I ordered my water from the bar and stayed there for the duration of a great battle waged by the 45 year old Bernard Hopkins. I my opinion, he won the fight but he was fighting a Canadian in Canada. They called it a draw but the punch stats did not concur.

The next morning at 7:00 AM, I headed back across the water to Belize City via the water taxi.

My flight wasn't until 1:20 PM, so I still had time to see some sights. Street taxi drivers are waiting for passengers to come off of the water taxi so transportation is not a problem. I still had about 4 hours before I needed to be at the airport so I did not rush to find the first available driver who approached me. I wanted to make sure I had the right driver with the knowledge of the history of Belize and also the right spirit to be with for the next few hours.

Just as I started to take a casual walk around the immediate area I was greeted by Cecil Gill who was perfect for the job. He greeted me with a friendly spirit and listened attentively as I expressed to him how I wanted to spend the next few hours. I highly recommend him as a tour guide for anyone seeking a responsible driver who has volumes of Belize history stored in his head. He also owns a scooter and bike rental service. After a great tour that included visits to some of the old churches, the Islamic school and Mosque, the Prime Ministers home and many other key locations, we headed for the airport. I went back home, after discovering new sights, tastes and even smells. I enjoyed myself and look forward to doing it again in the near future. This was indeed another great blessing in my life.

CHAPTER SEVEN

Vietnam - A Strange but Affordable Vacation Destination

I left Atlanta, GA on Monday but the flight left about five hours late so I missed the connection flight in Japan heading to Ho Chi Minh City (Saigon), in Vietnam.

So, since there is only one Al Nippon Airlines flight each day, I went to Hotel Nikko which was recommended by a lady that was also on the Atlanta flight. I paid $70.00 which not bad on such short notice.

The hotel is classy and has a free airport shuttle and a free shuttle to downtown Narita near the train station and I utilized both. I crashed hard that night even though I rode first class on Delta Airlines and slept many hours along the way. The next morning I got an early start and utilized the shuttle to explore a small part of Narita. I was dropped off by the shuttle bus and walked about a mile down a winding road that led to the Shinshoju Temple.

There are many temples and structures leading up to
the huge temple in the rear of the vast
property. Many Japanese come to pray and worship
the Fire God. I strolled around and took many
pictures before heading back to the shuttle bus
area. Along the walk I stopped at a few of the shops
that lined the winding street. Upon arrival back to
Hotel Nikko there was an airport shuttle just about
to leave so I jumped on it even though it got me to
the airport five hours early.

Be careful at the Narita airport because there is a south side and north side and travelers should be careful to position themselves in the proper area for their departure. Narita does have a free wifi service which I took advantage of before taking a nap. The flight to Ho Chi Minh City is six hours from Narita so I watched two movies and took another nap during the flight. Upon arrival I had to pay $45.00 US dollars to finalize my visa documents which must be provided at the counter in duplicate form. You must also bring two visa photos. I had filed the initial documents electronically for a $20.00 fee. The process took about 20 minutes.

My baggage never arrived so I filed a claim before getting a taxi to my hotel. The Bizu hotel, located at 183 De Tham Street, which I booked via booking.com, has free wifi and free breakfast and cost just $22.00 (473,000 Dong) per night. The location of the hotel is in District 1 which is the busiest district. The location is near the intersection of De tham and Bui Vien Streets which is in the heart of what the locals call "foreigner street".

There are cafés on the corners and a club just around the corner which plays loud music until about 4:00 am, so if you are looking for a party atmosphere and constant activity, then this is your place but if you're looking for a peaceful place, then select a different hotel. This area is filled with trash on the streets, vendors constantly hawking merchandise, a variety of stores, spas and restaurants and many tourists and backpackers strolling the streets. At night, as you walk the street, guys will likely be approached to purchase marijuana or sex. Some of those who approach you are "boy ladies", which are just dudes dressed like girls. Caution and awareness should be used to avoid being robbed by "boy ladies" or girls who may try to flirt and divert your attention in order to get your wallet or phone.

I heard one guy saying that a girl put her arm around him and then reached in his pocket and grabbed his phone. She then passed it to someone on a motorbike and they rode off. So even though there are many very nice people who live and work there, visitors should still be alert and aware of the bad apples.

The next morning my friend Byron, who had arrived a few days earlier and I got up early, ate a quick breakfast and boarded our bus en route to the Cu Chi Tunnels. The tour was arranged through our hotel and cost about $20.00 USD. The tunnels were used during the Vietnam War.

I learned the techniques the Vietnamese used that made them successful including living underground while fighting the war.

Photo by
A. Omar Muhammad (c) 2013

We saw how "boobie" traps and mines were set to
fight off US troops. We also saw a tank that had
been taken over by the Vietnamese. Many of the
Vietnamese soldiers were women. There were 16
thousand people living underground at that time and
the tunnels were complete with kitchens and water
wells. This was a great educational trip that should
not be missed.

Once we returned to Ho Chi Minh City, we stopped at the Ben Thanh Market to get some t-shirts and other souvenir's. The market is a huge draw for tourists and is in a central location. When traveling, this would also be a good area to book a hotel near this market, which would put you right in the thick of things and just a few blocks of the party zone or "Foreigner Street". You could also walk to other attractions such as the Central Post Office, the Notre Dame Cathedral, City Opera House and the higher end hotels and shopping areas.

Later that night after dinner we visited the Eden Spa, located at 57 Bui Vien Street in District 1, for a much needed pedicure which cost about $5.00 USD. The pedicurist spent about an hour on my feet and I'm sure it was the best pedicure I ever had. The next stop was the Thai Spa located just around the corner on De Tham Street.

Again, I experienced the best service ever and never felt rushed getting this massage which lasted over and hour and only cost about $5.00.

The next day after breakfast, we headed out to the area known as Chinatown. Just take the number one bus on Tran Hung Dao Street away from the Ben Thanh Market all the way to the last station stop. It's about a 30 minute ride and cost $5,000 DONG (25 cents USD). Here you can save even more money if you are willing to buy one dozen of that item. This is a wholesale market but the will sell individual items at a higher price. If you have many t-shirts to buy, then this would be a great place to shop. After the market visit we boarded the number one bus and headed back to the Ben Thanh Market area which is the last station stop in that direction.

We walked over to Mosque Musulman on Dong Du Street for Fridays Jumu'ah Prayer service. We were early so we decided to eat at the Halal Saigon Restaurant which is directly across the street. I ordered ginger chicken and rice and also ordered a dish of eggplant.

The food was delicious and highly recommended. The meal costs about 200,000 DONG (about $10.00 USD).

Photo by
. Omar Muhammad (c) 2013

The next morning I got up ready for my next
tour. This was a two day trip to the Mekong Delta,
which is about three hours south of Saigon. The tour
was arranged by Kim Travel and fulfilled by Delta
Adventure Tours located at 267 De Tham Street, just
down the street from my hotel. The bus ride was a
good opportunity for me to catch up on some sleep
that I missed the night before due to the loud music
from the club that I could hear in my fourth floor
hotel room. This tour included a trip to the coconut
candy factory, boat excursions on the Delta in motor
boats and canoes, lunch, hotel stay for one night, a
visit to a rice factory and a noodle factory and finally
to see the Floating Market.

Though this market is not set up for tourists to come and purchase fruits and vegetables but it instead for the purpose of selling wholesale to Vietnamese people in order for them to go back to their respective areas to resell those items. A few boats were permitted to come alongside our boat so that we could sample and purchase a few items. I bought a fresh whole pineapple for 50 cent and a large mango for only 25 cent.

Photo by
A. Omar Muhammad (c) 2013

We got to the Xuan Mai hotel located at 17 Dien Bien Phu Street in Can Thou City about 7:00 pm. I shared a room with Glen from the UK and after resting up and taking a shower, we decided to go out and check out the neighborhood.

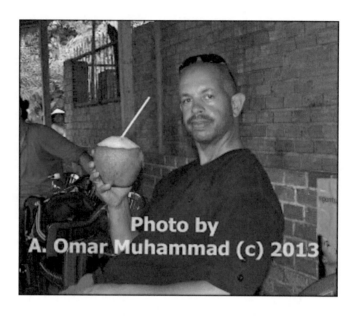

Photo by
A. Omar Muhammad (c) 2013

We ate at a small café and met Lan Huynh, the owner of a coffee shop called The Tiny Corner Café, who was also having dinner. She invited us to her coffee shop that was not far away on Ly Tu Trong Street and said they were having some entertainment that night. We did locate the shop with not too much difficulty and enjoyed the singing and music performed by some young amateur musicians before realizing that we were the last guests still there.

It was only about 11:30pm but the streets were. Can Thou City empty has a curfew and is not at all like Ho Chi Minh City (Saigon) and shuts down around 11:00pm.

I got up early the next morning to work out and connect with the neighborhood people. As I strolled down an intimate street a little girl ran up and hugged me. It seemed like she was familiar with the tourism trade but she was still very sweet. I took some pictures of her and gave her some money and it seemed like I was instantly accepted by those who witnessed the interaction.

I went on up the road to buy some tomatoes and a cucumber to eat for breakfast and headed back to the hotel. After we finished our excursion activities the next day, we headed back to Saigon about 2:00pm.

During our four hour trip back on this Sunday afternoon I noticed that, in blazing heat, everyone is working as if it is a weekday. Many Vietnamese will quickly tell you that they work seven days a week. I truly respect their grind and that's probably why even the hawkers don't really bother me much as they constantly run up on tourists selling shades, nail clips, combs, razors, bracelets, hats and anything else you can think of. There are of course some bad apples wherever you go, but in Vietnam, I see an overwhelming number of people who seem to have pride in working very hard.

When I arrived back I looked for another hotel room. I was not ready for another night of hearing music until 4:00 am. I was able to find a vacancy at the Thanh Thuong Guesthouse located at 241/6 Pham Ngu Lao Street, which is a tiny street that resembles an alley way.

Once you enter the alley, you find that there are a number of guesthouses, restaurants, stores and spas located along this passageway that leads to another main street on the other side. Thanh Thuong has free wifi, private rooms, hot showers and cable TV and only cost 315,000 Dong (15.00 USD) per night. It was also very quiet and the owners run a tight ship and pride themselves in keeping a reputable and secure place to stay. I got up early the next two mornings to work out in the park where exercise and dancing occurs daily starting at about 6:00 am. Many people seemed to enjoy having me there as I mixed in with the aerobic exercise groups and with those using the fixed exercise machines. I even jumped into some of the dancing classes. No gymnasium is required, just a willing spirit. The intense 90 degree heat seemed good for my body providing more flexibility. Even in the shade it felt like 80 degrees so I was sure to drink plenty of water. Students also workout in the park and some approached me to "practice English". I was honored by their request and was happy to accommodate them.

Afterwards I went to the VN Halai Restaurant located at 14 Pham Hong Thai and had some pineapple fish and rice which cost 115,00 DONG ($5.50 USD). I showered and went to the Dental Clinic NHA KHOA BEN THANH, for my 4:00 pm appointment that I had made earlier, to get my teeth whitened. They are located at 24 Pham Hong Thai which is across from the New World Hotel. The dental attendant also urged me to have my teeth cleaned first. The process took about two hours and cost 1,700,000 DONG ($80.00 USD).

My last day was peaceful. I worked out in the park once again and spoke to some of the people who appeared to be "regulars". After my workout I went to get a smoothie for 20,000 DONG ($1.00 USD) and went to check out of my hotel room. I also made m transportation arrangements for my return to the airport. The reservation was $9.00 USD and was set for 8:00 pm. I checked out some stores getting a few more souvenirs and got some fresh squeezed suge=ar cane juice from a cart vendor. I got a moterbike tour from Mosa who took me to see the Presidential Palace, the Post Office, the Notre Dame Cathedral and to Mosque Al Rahim where we had lunch before having prayer and heading back to Bui Vien Street. Mosa dropped me off in front of the Eden Spa so I could say farewell to my new friends.

My last stop was at an art shop called Little Oil at 114 Bui Vien St., where the store owner Tuyet Mai is the main artist. I bought two pieces of art and hurried off to my hotel to catch my 8:00 pm taxi to the airport. Vietnam was a great and affordable adventure trip and I look forward to going back to see so much more.

1.

I arrived in Narita at about 6:00 am and wasn't scheduled for my Atlanta connection until almost 4pm so I took advantage of the time and caught an express train into Tokyo just to have lunch and a massage (Japanese pronounce as "massage a"). Tokyo looked like the Wall Street area in New York with everyone in suits and ties walking swiftly through the streets. I hurried back to the train station en route back to the airport. The trip on the express train takes about one hour each way and be sure to get on the proper train. There are other trains that run from the Narita airport into Tokyo but they are not express trains so they take longer so if your time schedule is tight like my schedule was, then the correct train is critical. So plan ahead, do your research and enjoy. Peace and happy travels!.

CHAPTER EIGHT

Bangkok, Thailand, Must See at Least Once in a Lifetime

I used Thai Airways to get to Bangkok from Paris since I was already in Paris and they are one of Delta's partners and a member of the Sky Team. They had plenty of available seats on the A380 Airbus which can accommodate 276 passengers at once. The staff was quite accommodating as well, providing me with an Economy Comfort seat for this ten and a half hour flight. I took a quick nap on board even before the polite flight attendants served the meal consisting of chicken, snap peas and potatoes with smoked salmon and a light salad.

The meal also came with a custard dessert. The finely dressed attendants capture your attention with the bright colors of the traditional Thai styled attire.

I watched a movie called Savage during and after the meal about two guys that made lots of money selling marijuana and who shared the same girl. I took a nap afterwards and woke up to see that we were crossing the Caspian Sea so we were almost halfway to our destination. After going through customs I used an Airport Kiosk to book a room at the Diamond City Hotel, which is in the business area of Bangkok, not for from the famous MBK Mall. To get there, I took the Airlink train to the Phaya Thai stop and transferred to the Green Line Train to the Ratchathewi stop.

108

The Hotel is walking distance from there and the short stroll gives you a chance to get a good feel for Bangkok. The Hotel cost about $32 per night with free breakfast and free WiFi and the staff is very nice. There is a supermarket within walking distance. The indoor pool is smaller than the photos online and the water is very cold. The free breakfast was almost like eating dinner, complete with fried chicken, noodles, rice, mixed vegetables, eggs and toast. The hotel does require an additional $500 Baht deposit to hold for incidentals and returns it upon checkout.

After settling into the room it was time to explore the neighborhood so I headed over to the MBK Mall dropping my laundry off along the way to a local shop that only charged $50 Baht for my small load. I arrived at the MBK Mall to find a combination of Department stores and a giant flea market of activities. About five floors of vendors serving up an assortment of clothing and electronics with famous brand name products including; Nike, Adidas, Dr, Dre Beats headphones, i Phones, i Pads, Gucci bags and more, all at low prices.

There is also an assortment of restaurants for your dining pleasure within the mall. I headed back to the hotel in time for a 1:00 P.M tour around Bangkok that I scheduled at the Airport. It mainly consisted of a visit to the Reclining Buddha Temple. My tour guide, Nanzy also took me to James Fashion International which is well known Tailor Store that boasts clients worldwide. I must say that I was extremely impressed how they completed my tailor made two piece shirt and pant set in only six hours even though the craftsmanship was not perfect and my pinstriped lines in my material were not all lined up properly.

I designed the outfit and selected the material and they did the rest. By 9:00 p.m I had my outfit in hand. They are located at 439/1 Sukhothai Road, Suanchilada, Dubit, Bangkok. During my tour, we also rode through China Town. I got dropped off back at the MBK Mall where an outside concert was going on. It was a young group with high energy performing. After some additional shopping, I headed back to the hotel after a long day in the heat.

I used the hotel Internet then soaked my feet in cold water before turning in. I got up the next morning and enjoyed the complimentary breakfast buffet, went back to the MBK Mall, picked up my laundry and checked out of the hotel before the 12:00 Noon check out time. I took a taxi to the Century Mall where you can ride a comfortable van for the almost two hour ride to Pattaya for only $100 Baht or $3.00 USD.

Pattaya is the area where people go to enjoy the beach and nightlife so I had it on my list of things to do in Bangkok. The area I was in had a very small beach that was close to the street and not very appealing. Another highly sought after area is Phuket which is an island about 1 ½ hours away by air. I was told by both visitors and natives that if you really want to enjoy beautiful scenery and beaches then Phuket is the place to go.

I checked in to the Sabai Inn, at $42.00 USD per night, it's a nice hotel with free wifi, fridge and safe in a large room and within a five minute walk to the beach. The water in Pattaya was so warm it was like swimming in a sauna. The streets are filled with restaurants, tailor shops, and most of all bars and clubs where many escort girls hang out and make proposals to male tourists to buy drinks in the bars that they are posted up at. There are many street food vendors but I decided to keep it safe and eat at overpriced Sizzlers. I was later informed that the native food actually is very safe as long as the vendor keeps a clean food storage and cooking area.

I headed back to the Sabai Inn hotel to prepare for an early departure. I had a 5:55 am flight and was about 2 hours from the airport. The taxi fee was 1,600 baht which is about $50.00 USD. I had only spent about 48 hours in Bangkok so I know there is so much more to be discovered there. I look forward to going back one day to visit Phuket and some of the other beautiful areas in Thailand.

CHAPTER NINE

How to See Three Countries
in Five Days

The Magic of Spain

I escaped Hurricane Sandy, which was en-route to New Jersey on October 28, 2012, by first leaving Newark Airport and going to JFK where I was promised that I could board a flight to Atlanta, GA, which was my final destination. Things did not work out that way and the two flights that were said to be added on were also full and not allowing for any standby passengers like myself.

I understood from the start, seeing all of the chaos at the Airport with so many frantic passengers also trying to escape the effects of Hurricane Sandy, that I may not make it out to Atlanta.

With none of the connection options within the US looking good, I decided to check my international options. After checking international destinations that were not so popular like Mexico City and Brussels, Madrid came up with the most available seats in First Class, so I went for it. If you're going to ride for many hours, you may as well ride comfortably.

I was supposed to land at about 9:30 A.M and take the 10:50 A.M flight to Atlanta, GA, but we were late leaving JFK due to the many planes that were waiting in a single line to take off due to the storm that was approaching. So stranded in Madrid was not bad considering I could have been stuck in New York or New Jersey in storm related conditions. I checked into the Auditorium Hotel which is about 10 minutes from the Airport. It is a beautiful hotel with many rooms, free Wi-Fi, breakfast and Airport shuttle. Room prices start at about $68.00 euros. Taxis are readily available outside and local buses also stop in front. I took the bus to Aveinedo De. American which is a popular business area and is also a Metro Train Station. I walked around the area to get a feel for Madrid, went to an Internet Cafe and had a salad at the Hontanares Cafe. I went back to the Metro Station and headed to Sol which is the city center and has many shopping opportunities and many activities and entertainers in the courtyard area. Take the number four train to the Goyas stop, then take the number two train to Sol.

This is a very popular tourist area and the talented street entertainers including Human Statues and even a Mariachi Band will keep you busy for hours. I enjoyed people watching as I sat while a young man from Mali gave me a desperately needed shoe shine. I did some window shopping, bought a hat to protect me from the cool night air, then headed back to the Hotel. I spent the rest of the night researching ways to leave Madrid the next day. But because I had now enjoyed some of the beauty of Madrid, I would not be disappointed if I could not get out. I got up the next morning and had a great complimentary buffet breakfast in one of the hotels fine restaurants before heading to the Airport to continue my journey. I felt good about my detour to Madrid abd even look forward to returning and spending more time there. A few things I would likely do again would be to visit Sol and stay at the Hotel Auditorium. As I continue on to Geneva and then to Amsterdam, I know that there is much more to discover in Madrid.

The Adventures of Amsterdam

My short unexpected two day stay in Amsterdam was pleasant, despite the cold weather. From the Shipol Airport you will find plenty of trains and buses to take you to your desired location. I booked two different Guest Houses during my stay but would only recommend one of them. The StayOkay Guest House has everything you would need for a comfortable, safe and inexpensive stay. The dorm I shared was about $24 US dollars per person. They have free WiFi and free breakfast. They also have safes for your valuables for a small additional fee. It is close to Museums, the Holland Casino and "The Square" which is a very good strategic location for trams and buses. The other great area to be in is what is called the City Center, a very large courtyard is surrounded by shops, large historic buildings that resemble castles, and eateries. The Metro Train Station is also close by. The Red Light District is also in this area. The main Supermarket is called Albert Hein.

121

I attempted to leave Amsterdam and go to Bangkok the next day but was unsuccessful. The StayOkay Guest House was sold out so I had to find another room. The Marnix was close the the Square but was a bit depressing compared to the StayOkay. Free WiFi but no free breakfast and a bunch of young guys smoking weed and spitting all over the stairway that lead to the rooms. The young fellas were very friendly as many people in Amsterdam are, but then weed smoking tends to make people friendly. The "Coffee Shops" are the places where people go to legally smoke the various brands of marijuana offered. I left the Marnix and headed to the Square. Before booking the train, I stopped at the Pancake Restaurant (to have a pancake of course). The pancake is more like a crepe the size of the entire plate. It was tasty and really doesn't need syrup even though it is available.

Buying clothes could be an expensive venture as I did not see any real discounts. I bought a scarf for four euros and that was it. So as I headed to Paris, I looked forward to seeing what would contrast from what I experienced during my short stay in Amsterdam.

2.

One Night in Paris

I arrived in Paris from Amsterdam thinking that the outside temperature would be a bit warmer, but actually to my surprise it actually felt colder. I went to the information desk right away to see the best option to get transportation to my Hotel. They directed me to the Air France bus area. There you will find a number of different bus stops corresponding to the various destinations that Air France offers.

They are not only in the flying business, but also in the ground transportation business. The fare to go from the Airport to Paris in these comfortable charter type buses is 29 euros round trip for a one hour ride. There are only two stops on the bus, one at Port Maillot, (and one at Charles DeGaille) which is a large courtyard area with large statues and Museums. You can also walk from there to see the Eiffel Tower of you can catch the number six metro train for just a few stops. My inexpensive hotel was about 33 Euros for a private room. The name was Hotel De Nantes (pronounced Di Not) and I must say they "DI NOT "have an elevator, and my room was on the sixth floor. They "DI NOT" have much heat at all and they "DI NOT" have a room that did not smell like an ash tray. They did however offer free WiFi and the reception person was pleasant, but my recommendation would be, do not stay at De Nantes. I left early the next morning so I could go and take some photos of the Eiffel Tower and then make my way to the Airport.

Au Revoir Paris!

CHAPTER TEN

The Challenges of Traveling to India

Before I even boarded the first leg of my trip to India I faced
incredible tasks in preparation of my journey. United States
residents must first obtain a visa prior to traveling. The India
Consulate outsources the processing of visas to a company
called Travisa. Georgia residents, like myself, are instructed to
use the Travisa office located in Houston, Texas.

Since I planned to leave for India as soon as possible, I decided
to hop a flight to Houston to fast-track my processing. I got the
first flight out of Atlanta and arrived at the Houston Hobby
Airport around 9:00 am for my 10:00 am appointment. Travisa
accepts applications in person, from 9:00 to 11:00 am. The taxi
ride was about 30 minutes and cost me $45.00. My plan was to
deliver my application and supporting documents, go out on
the town for a few hours, pick up my passport complete with
my new visa for India and head back to the airport to fly back
home. Well, things did not quite go that smoothly.

I did not realize that the pick-up time for documents is not until 5:30 pm to 6:00 pm and by that time I was a good distance across town. When I called the office around 4:00 pm they could not assure me that my passport would be ready that same day so I paid an additional $22.00 to have the visa mailed via Fed Ex.

I had already missed the last flight back to Atlanta so I decided to check into a Fairfield Inn located in Humble, TX, at a rate of about $75.00, which had a great indoor pool and sauna that I utilized after I took a short walk to a nearby mall to "get my feet done". That's how guys say getting a pedicure. A callus on the ball of my foot was giving me some major pain. The hotel also offered free use of the internet accessible computer workstation which was very helpful as I needed to check the status of flights leaving the George Bush International Airport which was about 10 minutes from the hotel. After I enjoyed the complimentary breakfast, I prepared to take three separate flights to make my way back to Atlanta. This was my best option since I fly standby. I didn't have my visa yet but my feet felt much better and I was heading home.

It was Labor Day weekend so I knew I could not expect my passport back before Tuesday. Well, Tuesday rolled around and still no Fed Ex delivery. I changed my flight plans for a Wednesday departure. I did receive an email stating that my visa was approved. On Wednesday the waiting game continued.

I had rescheduled myself for the 3:00 pm flight to Boston, MA where I would connect to the 7:00 pm flight to Amsterdam. There was an Atlanta to Amsterdam flight but it did not look as though it would have any available seats. From Amsterdam I planned to catch the 10:20 am flight to Mumbia, India which would arrive around 11:00 pm. Thursday night. From there my plan was to catch an early Friday morning flight to Chennai, India. I had to pay the full round trip fare to go to Chennai since Delta did not fly there.

The Fed Ex delivery came at 2:00 pm, just around the time I almost threw in the towel for the day. I opened the envelope and within five minutes I was in my car racing to the airport. I wanted to keep my current plans because the flights did not look good the following day and I had already booked a room in Chennai for my first night based on my expected arrival on Friday.

I arrived at the airport about 2:50 pm. It was too late to check my large suitcase which was full of water, juices and a small food supply. All bags need to be checked in about an hour before flight time so I left my large bag in the car. I only took along my small carry-on luggage which had all of my essentials. I had also printed out my boarding pass but since it did not scan properly, the TSA operator asked me to go to the counter to get another copy.

Once that was done, my mini marathon began. I shuffled through the line, announcing and pleading "can I go ahead of you, I have a 3:10 pm flight". Everyone was very accommodating as I scurried along even forgetting to take my sneakers off or take my phone out of my pocket as I attempted to pass by the TSA security check.

By this time it was about 3:00 pm and I still had to take the "plane train" for one stop to Concourse A. I ran up the escalator and through the concourse lobby and actually made it to the gate with a few minutes to spare. Incredible!

There were many open seats in coach but first class was full going to Boston. I arrived on time but the flight to Amsterdam was delayed by one hour. When the standby seats were assigned I was happy to be in business class seat 4F for this six to seven hour flight. I enjoyed the comfortable seat and tasty food that was served on this Delta flight. I selected the chicken, mashed potatoes and artichokes that also came with a side salad and fresh fruit for dessert.

We arrived in Amsterdam and I had to move swiftly to transfer to my next flight. I used the kiosk to get my seat request, answered a few questions about my final destination and hotel plans and was then treated to a business class seat (1F). I prepared myself for another wonderful Delta flight.

The cuisine choices included vegetarian and non-vegetarian Indian food. Both selections included black lentil masala, sautéed spinach with chilli and basmati rice.

The non-veggy meal also included butter chicken curry. The appetizers included a stuffed tomato (stuffed with chickpeas and mushroom bhaji), cream of onion soup and fresh mesclun salad. Just the menu alone had me excited about the trip.

Photo by A. Omar Muhamm

Once I arrived in Mumbai I purchased a roundtrip ticket to Chennai for $305.00. The International and Domestic Terminals in Mumbai are housed in two separate buildings and are about twenty minutes apart. There are large charter type buses that provide free transportation from one terminal to the other. The domestic terminal check in area is inviting with airlines such as Indigo, Jet Airways, Spicejet, prominently displayed.

Many guards are visible but security may be effective due to the high visibility as opposed to functional and operational effectiveness of the guards.

Photo by
A. Omar Muhammad (c) 2012

After landing, I headed toward the exit and booked a prepaid taxi for $380.00 rupees to take me to my hotel. That way, I wouldn't have to worry about a "meter gone wild" or a taxi driver just trying to get overpaid. The ride was about 45 minutes long in an older model vehicle made in India called the Ambassador. We arrived at Priyadarshini Park Hotel, which is a dimly lit, one or two star hotel, that I would not recommend even though the staff was very nice. The room was clean but they had no pool or gym and the free breakfast was mediocre. The best thing about this hotel was the location which was just across from the Government Secretariat building and the train station. The Makeah Mosque was also just down the road. They also had free wifi which was a big plus but many other hotels also offer both free breakfast and wifi.

I took a short four hour tour offered by the hotel travel desk. The driver was very cordial as he drove me around but when I went to the mosque he stayed with the car. I left my bag containing my camera, ID and money in the trunk. This proved to be a big mistake. Be sure when taking tours to make sure the driver is aware that when you leave the vehicle, that they must also exit the vehicle. I did not realize the money was missing until I was back in my hotel room. I reported the incident to the travel desk but he did not seem at all concerned. I just hope my money went to good use.

The next day I decided to walk to the Spencer Mall, which is four floors of stores situated in a maze of activity. Be sure to visit the Indian Art Gallery (4th floor), Eves's and Chinar (both on the 1st floor). You can strike up many bargains at this mall and I recommend never agreeing to the first price quoted. I made some pretty good deals on gifts for my family and also made contacts for future orders. Keep in mind that 1000 rupees equals about $18.00 US dollars. I spent the entire day at this mall and afterwards was treated by Mohammed Sayed to a great dinner at the Palmshore Restaurant, consisting of grilled Basa fish and side vegetables. So far my stomach was holding up fine. I had been warned about foreigners going to India and getting sick after eating the food. Sayed also invited me to a wedding the following day.

I checked out of my hotel and checked into the Raj Park Hotel the following morning . It was a great move and a few steps up. They had a pool, a gym, free breakfast with good food, free wifi and the hotel was clean. The shower was great with hot water and the room was gorgeous. I should have stayed there exclusively for my entire stay. The staff was very efficient but not exactly warm and inviting.

I couldn't resist accepting the invitation to the wedding after Sayed told me there would be about two-thousand guests. This was an arranged which is quite common in the Indian culture. This was the fourth day of a five day wedding celebration. The males all congregated in a huge hall and the females next door in a separate hall. The groom and bride did not see each other but instead engaged in separate ceremonies. Afterwards, there was a feast that consisted mostly of Biryani, which was a spicy rice dish with lamb mixed in. It was served on a mat with no eating utensils. The right hand is used to eat, which makes sense since I saw many Indians publicly digging in their noses, but always with their left hands. Well this spicy mat full of Biryani proved to be my dietary downfall, which was manifested after I went back to my hotel and fell asleep only to wake up around 4:00 am with terrible stomach pains. As I ran back and forth to the bathroom, praying to the Indian "spice gods" I knew that my journey back home that would start in a few hours, would not be enjoyable.

I arranged for my transportation to the airport and decided see a few more sights on the way to the airport. I paid $1,600.oo rupees for four hours of service. The airport was only about an hour away. The driver was supposed to take me to the beach, a few temples and other points of interest and get me to the airport around 1:30pm. We left the hotel at 9:45am and only stopped at the beach and one temple then he headed to the airport. We arrived at the airport at 11:00 am so I only received 1 hour and fifteen minutes of service when I paid for four hours. The driver was asking me about his tip long before we ever got to the airport. When we arrived he started asking again about his tip. I told him it was rude for him to ask me especially since he did not provide the services that I paid for.

The lesson I learned was to stick with a reputable tour company instead of using the hotel driver especially if it is for specialized service requests.

I saw in Chennai, India, a place with so many people who live in poverty, some not even wearing shoes or sandals. I saw a place that has obvious disparities in wealth between the "havs" and "have-nots". I saw barefoot cement workers repairing the street. I saw children walking the streets without shoes and I saw many, many beggars.

I also saw a peaceful culture with co-existence between Hindus and Muslims. I saw women who did not dress in sexually suggestive ways but instead kept their bodies covered in public. I saw the sensibility of using motorcycles, mopeds and tuk-tuks (three wheelers) as the regular means of transportation to cut down on the number of cars on the streets.

This journey was thrilling and mostly good (except for the Biryani) and I will cherish the opportunity I had to go there, ALWAYS!

CHAPTER ELEVEN

Visit Sydney Australia for a Worthwhile Adventure

Photo by
A. Omar Muhammad (c) 2012

From Atlanta, GA I flew about five hours into the Los Angeles Airport and then another fifteen hours to Sydney Australia. Since I fly standby with Delta, I was hoping to get a first class seat for this lengthy flight but unfortunately it didn't happen. I was assigned an economy comfort seat which helped since the seat reclines a bit more than the regular coach seats and there is also a little more leg room, but I guess at this point I am spoiled and when traveling more than four hours, I just really want to stretch all the way out and lay flat down to sleep. I slept sporadically, watched a few movies and got up numerous times to stretch my back and legs but overall I enjoyed the trip. I found out a few days before my trip that my schoolmate Lachelle had moved to Sydney some 24 years ago and she was happy to pick me up from the airport. She and her life partner Kat along with daughter Nayeli live in the Summer Hill section so after leaving my bags at their place we took the train to Bondi beach, one of Sydney's famous attractions.

After enjoying the great scenery at the beach, we took a bus to Watson's Bay which is a well-known area and the place where you can find the very popular Doyle's Restaurant.

The next day I checked into the Sydney South Waldorf Apartments in the Chippendale area near the Redfern train station. The one bedroom apartments are $174.00 per night and can accommodate four people. This worked out great since I was sharing the apartment with two of my coworkers (LaShunda and Anita) and LaShunda's mother Betsy.

We took the rail car to Circular Quay (pronounced Circular KEY) which is the hub for ferries, buses and the CityRail trains then took the Captain Cook ferry about 15 minutes over to Taronga Zoo which was a wonderful experience.

I saw elephants, giraffe, alligators, reptiles and also enjoyed the seal show and the bird show. Afterwards we all went to the Millennium Pizzeria at 103 Cleveland Street and had a delicious Melanzane pizza complete with eggplant, parmesan, garlic and roast capsicum (green peppers). Afterwards, Lachelle and Kat came to visit and the night was complete.

My third day in Sydney was also great. We took the train to Blacktown, which is about an hour ride going west from Circular Quay. We then took another train to Katoomba where we picked up the Hop on Hop off bus that rode a route around the Blue Mountain area. This is one of the most fascinating scenes you will see when visiting Sydney. We took a sky lift across from one side of the mountain to the other. With a waterfall far down in the valley and the famous Three Sisters rock formations set along one side of the mountain, you are sure to be amazed and in awe. We also had the opportunity to ride the world's steepest railcar which is said to be 52 degrees going down.

We again boarded the bus and stopped at one of the easier hiking locations. The brochure was very descriptive and rated each stop along the route as being easy, moderate or difficult and also stated the approximate time it would take to complete the hike. Even on our "easy" hike there were many steps to climb down, and then back up. After our hike we headed back to the train station for our journey back to Sydney. Once we got back to the apartment we all realized just how exhausting the trip was and it made for an early night.

Photo by
A. Omar Muhammad (c) 2012

LaShunda, Anita and Betsy headed to the airport the next morning and I went back to Lachelle and Kat's house. From there, I headed to Manly beach using the train from Summer Hill to Circular Quay then boarding the Ferry.

I had a multi ticket which means you can ride the train, the bus and some ferries using the same ticket. If you travel to Sydney and are staying for four or more days it would be smart to purchase a weekly multi-pass ticket. The transportation system is very good for natives and tourists who want to move around the many areas of Sydney and the outer suburbs. Manly beach is a very popular attraction in Sydney. The main street leading to the beach is lined with clothing and souvenir shops along with many eateries along the strip. There were many teenagers along the beach as schools were closed for what is called "Holiday".

I used the afternoon to relax as I watched the swimmers and surfers. The water was still too cold for me to jump in even though I was tempted. I did manage to walk along the edge to get my feet wet and even that gave me the chills. I made my way back to the house and enjoyed the meal Kat prepared consisting of salmon, baked potato and asparagus.

I went to Featherdale Wildlife Park the next morning with Kat and Nayeli. The park is located at 217 Kildare road in Doonside. It is accessible by public transportation by taking the train to the Blacktown station and then take the #725 bus.

Photo by
A. Omar Muhammad (c) 2012

If you are on a tight schedule and cannot fit in the time to go to Taronga Zoo, which is a much larger zoo, then go to Featherdale because it is smaller but has many different animals, birds and reptiles, all in close proximity so you can move around quickly as you see penguins, pelicans, kangaroo, birds and more.

You can even watch a crocodile devour his food at feeding time. They also have a petting area with sheep and goat that really holds the attention of the children.

Kat dropped me off at the Town Hall station and from there I went to another hot spot in Sydney called Kings Cross. This is the red light district and at night it is said to be filled with prostitutes and other elements of the night. Above some of the bars there are some of the many hostels that are plentiful in this area, which is more suitable for the younger crowd.

I took a few photos, walked around the neighborhood, visited a book store and then decided I saw enough. It was still early so I guess the real excitement would not get started until later that night. I already had plans for the night which included a show at a place called The Basement, which is located at 7 Macquarie Place, Circular Quay. I had read about the show while preparing for the trip to Sydney and had included it on my tentative itinerary. Performing was Afro Moses O'Jah and his thirteen piece band and the show fulfilled all of my expectations. I became familiar with the Afrobeats sound in Atlanta when I went to hear the dynamic Roy Ayers perform with the energetic group, Common Ground Collective. I figured the Afro Moses O'Jah would provide a similar sound and he indeed delivered. Lachelle and I had a great time that night as Afro Moses got nearly the entire room full of people on the dance floor. He dedicated the show to his mother who had recently passed away.

My Sunday activities the next day included going to Redfern to try and locate some of the Indigenous people who live in that area but upon arrival to the area where they lived, I only saw the vacant land that they were forced to move from by the government. I spoke to a few ladies who said that it was her ancestors land and that it was stolen from them. She said the government provides them with food but the land was taken away.

I took the train to Circular Quay and took a ferry to Darling Harbor which is a dock lined with pricey restaurants and great views. I ate at the Cyren restaurant and only had a pizza and water and my tab was still about $50.00. For the more budget conscious tourists your best bet is to walk a few blocks to the Chinatown area where there are numerous restaurants lining the street. The well-known Haymarket is also adjacent to Chinatown and has some of the best souvenir bargains that you will find in Sydney. I finished off my walk and headed to the Queen Victoria building about a half mile away, looked around at some of the great architecture and then headed in after a full day.

The next day was Monday and I was supposed to be heading to the airport but decided to stay another day. This gave me a chance to interview my friend Lachelle, who is an amputee and had some very interesting things to say about the medical industry in the USA versus the one in Australia. (Listen out for the interview on my Youtube channel entitled Omar the Traveler.

After the interview I went to the Central Rail Station and walked to Hyde Park where they had an Arts Festival. I walked through the park taking photos of the art displays, the many gardens and unique trees. I made my way over to St. Mary's Cathedral to check out the fine architecture.

I then walked around the Opera House, which is one of the top attractions in Sydney.

I had also wanted to visit a mosque while in Sydney and this extra day afforded me the opportunity. I met with Nagima, who I was introduced to by Lachelle at The Basement. She is a remarkable woman from Zimbabwe and came to Australia as a refugee. She knew about a mosque in a suburb called Auburn so we took the train to the Auburn Station and met Abdul who was from Pakistan and he accompanied us to the beautiful Gallipoli Mosque. After we had prayer we talked for a while and headed back to Sydney.

With this final day under my belt I now felt like my trip was complete. I had a great time in Sydney, seeing all of the great attractions including the Taronga Zoo, the Blue Mountains, the Bondi and Manly Beaches and best of all enjoying the company of old and new friends. As I flew 7,500 miles back to Los Angeles fully reclined in my comfortable Delta first class seat, I knew this was one of my greatest adventures yet. I thought Australia would be a one-time visit but I am already looking forward to another visit there especially to see my old and now new friends.

CHAPTER TWELVE

Travel to Dubai for a Trip to a Desert Wonderland

Many people want to make the journey to Dubai to experience the rich heritage and great visual wonders to behold in the vast desert areas, not to mention the opportunity to get a great deal on the gold jewelry and to visit the tallest building in the world. It is also home to the Emirates Mall which houses an amazing ski resort attraction inside of the mall complete with a ski lift and plenty of snow to play with.

The United Arab Emirates (UAE) is the formal name of this desert wonderland where Islam is the dominant religion and culture which is apparent upon your arrival at the Dubai International Airport. My daughter was surprised when she was approached by a female security officer who instructed her that public gum chewing was not permitted. I smiled as I reflected on memories of me telling her that chewing in public was uncivilized. You will also see many men and women in fully garbed robes and garments. While critics may disagree with the strict rules they cannot argue with the low crime rate in Dubai which is directly related to their stringent regulations.

My family did some research to find an affordable and accessible hotel and found a gem right near the airport. The Premier Inn was around $79.00 per night which totaled, with taxes, around $285.00 for three nights. They have a complimentary shuttle bus service that runs to the airport and to the Metro train station every 30 minutes. They also have free WiFi in every room, a beautiful rooftop swimming pool and Jacuzzi. The restaurant serves great food and for a nominal fee you can enjoy a buffet breakfast. There are also local restaurants that deliver food to the hotel. We used the Century Express Restaurant to satisfy our children's craving for pizza. They also have chicken, fish and salads on their menu. Restaurant menus are available from the hotel receptionist.

The Metro train is a great way to see many places in Dubai including the Emirates Mall and the world's tallest building.

My family couldn't wait to get into the ski resort area of the mall. Admission to that attraction is about $70.00 per person but offers a memory of a lifetime. I decided instead to go check out a movie in the mall theater while they played in the snow. The temperature outside was about 110 degrees so I wasn't quite ready for the cold.

We left the mall and went to the Burj Khalifa which is commonly known as the world's tallest building. The ground floor of the Burj Khalifa is also a mall filled with many restaurants and stores. Visitors can pay about $18.00 to go up to the 124th floor for a great view of Dubai and another experience of a lifetime.

The next day we planned a Safari tour that included an exciting ride in the desert in four wheel drive trucks. This part of the excursion resembled a roller coaster ride as we went up and down the many sand hills in a five-truck caravan of Toyotas. You may want to skip having any food before this up and down ride. In the outdoor waiting area prior to going we saw exotic birds and some monkeys.

After the Dune ride we went to the next part of the tour which was the camel ride an exciting live show with dancers wearing colorful and illuminated outfits.

The experience of riding a camel is amazing even though they are carefully guided by the workers who escort them in the staged area. It's the kind of thing that you want to do at least once in your lifetime.

The dancers were great and entertained us as we ate. The costumes were so colorful as the darkness of the night drew in, the costumes lit up and made the event even more festive. The buffet is also a great part of the tour and includes some exotic foods. Be sure to hurry and get your fill of food before they shut the buffet down prior to the end of the tour schedule. The tour lasts for about four hours and costs about $70.00 per person. The drive back to our hotel was over an hour so it gave us time to reflect on our great experience and to relax.

Another way to enjoy the culture in Dubai is to find a restaurant that the locals dine at regularly. We found a great place with the help of a taxi driver. If you want great affordable food when you travel just ask the taxi drivers where they eat.

The food was fantastic at the Karachi Darbar Restaurant and the prices were very reasonable with entrees ranging from $5.00 to $12.00 in US money. You may also use the Dirham which is the money that is commonly used but US dollars are accepted in some places.

My family had a fabulous time in Dubai and will always cherish the opportunity that we had to go there. It is a place that is still growing as they are even creating space by building on areas that was once occupied by water!

CHAPTER THIRTEEN

Niagara Falls Via Toronto

I wondered how I would spend the anniversary of my birthday and since my family was in St. Louis visiting my son I thought I would do something that I always wanted to do but would not cost much money. I had just visited St. Louis a few weeks ago so I decided that Niagara Falls was a good choice. This was confirmed when a gentleman from Canada came into the International Airport and checked in at the Delta counter where I work. I asked him about Canada and the Falls. He said it would make a great trip but advised me to go on the Canadian side instead of seeing the Falls from the New York side. He said that even though it would be less expensive going from the Buffalo, NY airport,

I would likely not like the environment and hotels which he described as "dingy". He said it was much cleaner on the Canadian side. So even though I had done research and had prepared my commute from the Buffalo Airport I decided to take his advise and began researching hotels and transportation services from the Toronto Airport (YYZ).

My total expenses for my one night stay in Toronto cost me about $200.00 including hotel, transportation and food. I traveled by bus once I arrived at the airport. I took an express bus that picked me up at the airport and dropped me off at the bus station located at 610 Bay Street in downtown Toronto for $40.00 round trip. I then purchased a round trip ticket to the Niagara Falls bus station that costs $35.00. Once I got there I took a local bus for about two miles and cost $5.00 round trip. So, for $80.00 I covered all of my bus fees for the trip, which was about two hours each way.

This worked out great for me especially since the Holiday Inn Express on Dixon Road that I selected was close to the airport and provided a free shuttle service. The room had a king size bed, was clean and the staff was friendly. They also had a great looking pool and Jacuzzi which I didn't have time to enjoy.

I got a great deal on Hotwire.com using the 50% off on "mystery" 3 star hotels tab and only paid $71.00 including all taxes. My only other expenses was food which came to about $50.00.

Once I arrived near the Falls on the local bus, I walked through two blocks of entertainment venues including places like Ripley's Believe It or Not, restaurants and shops and there it was... beautiful streams of water and crowds of people everywhere! I took many photos and enjoyed watching the boats full of people wanting to get an "up close and personal" view of the falls. They were all equipped with rain gear for these tours that carried them very close to going under the falls. I decided to stay dry and remain a spectator. Besides, I did not want to take a chance getting my Nikon D200 wet.

There are other options to travel to the Falls including the GO Train which leaves from Union Station in Toronto and arrives at the Niagara Falls Train Station at 4267 Bridge Street and costs about $80.00 round trip. The additional costs would be a taxi to get to the stations.

I would like to go back to this beautiful and picturesque place but next time with my entire family including cousins. They would really enjoy the area near the falls and all of the entertainment venues that it has to offer and they may even look over at the Falls and reflect on the beauty of nature and feel the way I did... BLESSED.

CHAPTER FOURTEEN

Philippines - The Perfect October Getaway for Beach Lovers

Photo by A. Omar Muhammad (c) 2011

Late October is not an easy time to find the perfect beach getaway. I searched many destinations only to find that they were being hammered with showers and cloudy skies. Many had forecasts showing a 60-80% chance of rain. Other places, like Madrid, Paris and Capetown were only getting temperatures of about 60-65 degrees. Not hardly warm enough for those like me, who love the beach.

Santo Domingo in the Dominican Republic did show 80 degree weather and only a 30% chance of rain but since I had just recently visited there, I decided that Manila in the Phillipines would be a great choice.

The flight left Atlanta, GA at 1:45pm and landed in Tokyo Japan the next day about 5:15pm. I then boarded another flight to Manila which takes about four hours. I looked forward to seeing the sights in Manila and also visiting the neighboring island of Boracay, which I read so much about online. Boracay boasts of its white sand beaches and claims to be one of the best beaches in the world.

Photo by A. Omar Muhammad (c) 2011

I arrived in Manila about 10:00 pm, exchanged some money and took a taxi for 250p ($5.00) to the Oasis Park Hotel, which is located in the hood but not very far from Makita, which is a very built up area. The hotel was only $37.00 per night and located next to a larger hotel.

I was greeted very kindly upon my arrival, received a complimentary beverage ticket and shown to my room, located in this four story older model hotel that had no elevator. Thankfully I was on the 3rd floor instead of the fourth. The room was fair but the water only trickled out of the shower. I could not get a signal to use the internet in my room as promised and had to go down to the bar area to go online. I used the opportunity to cash in my free drink ticket and got a pineapple/cranberry juice mixture. I must say that even though the price is very low, I would not recommend this hotel to anyone. You can likely find other hotels in this same price range.

Using the internet was vital because I had to plan my next moves, including how I would travel to Boracay island and where I would stay once I arrived. Two of the options for getting to the island are either flying or taking a van then a ferry boat. The flight takes about one hour while the van and boat take about 20 hours. The round-trip flight cost $200.00 - $300.00 while the van and boat cost about $25.00. The van and boat trip also occurs during the night, so some people may not be comfortable with that option. I opted for the flight on Cebu Pacific Airlines at a cost of $300.00 roundtrip which I booked the same day as my flight. If you search the internet and purchase tickets in advance, you can easily find flights for around $200.00 or less.

I checked out of the Oasis and headed to the airport for my 2:30pm flight to Caticlan airport. That is the closest airport to the island. The flight was delayed and the waiting area was packed like sardines. After arriving about 4:15pm I got a mortorized tricycle to the dock for 20p.

Other fees besides the ferry cost must be paid prior to boarding which include an environmental fee and a terminal fee. The ferrys are fairly small, carrying a maximum of 50 people or less at a time. It is a short 20-30 minute ride to Boracay Island. The beach area is divided into three stations and knowing which station your hotel is located in will help the driver get you to your destination. You can take a van, taxi or motorized tricycle. The tricycle will always be the most cost effective.

I checked in to the Casa Pilar Hotel which is situated right on the beach in station. The rooms are small cottages that are all on the ground level. The room rate was $48.00 per night which is not bad even though they did not have complimentary wifi. That amenity is really not needed due to the many restaurants along the strip that offer it free.

The strip runs adjacent to the 1 1/2 mile beach and is lined with many businesses, shops and vendors of all types. Tourists and local provide non-stop viewing for the avid people watchers. At night you can hear many different musicians and DJ's vying for the attention of the passersby. Halloween is becoming a big holiday in the Phillipines and many bars offer costumed themes and parties during the end of October.

I took a late dip in the calm waters of the Pacific since the evening temperature was still above 70 degrees. Many people seem to avoid the water during the day when the sun is scorching at 85 degrees. The bands and music played late into the night until about 3:00 am. The next day I got some sun on the beach went to a buffet which costs 250P ($5.00 US

The strip runs adjacent to the 1 1/2 mile beach and is lined with many businesses, shops and vendors of all types. Tourists and local provide non-stop viewing for the avid people watchers. At night you can hear many different musicians and DJ's vying for the attention of the passersby.

Halloween is becoming a big holiday in the Phillipines and many bars offer costumed themes and parties during the end of October. I took a late dip in the calm waters of the Pacific since the evening temperature was still above 70 degrees. Many people seem to avoid the water during the day when the sun is scorching at 85 degrees. The bands and music played late into the night until about 3:00 am.

Water sports are also available including banana boat rides, scuba diving, jet ski and other water activities. I had to get settled and get on the computer to plan my next moves. I had an early 6:50 am flight the next day and since the ferry did not start running until 5:00 am, I wanted to research that subject online to see if others also had any scheduling issues with early flights.

    I checked out of the hotel about 4:00 am and made it to the ferry with time to spare. When I got to the airport in Caticlan, they weren't even open yet. I was in great shape for my flight back. Once again there were additional fees to pay. I even had to pay 480P ($10.00 US) to check my bag which is normally a carry on. It wasn't much but when your used to your carry on being free of charge it is a bit unsettling.

Once I was back in Manila I went to the Mall of Asia which is not far away. The taxi service cost 250P ($5.00 US) to get me there. My plan was to take a city tour using the Hop-On, Hop-Off bus, which advertised a pick up location at the mall. The bus never came but I had used the waiting time to research nearby hotels using the Mall of Asia's free wi-fi zone.

I took a taxi to the Victoria Court Hotel which was very close and very affordable. The room cost 1,650P ($30.00US) and was immaculate! They also had free internet and their service was very professional. This hotel is highly recommended by me for location, quality of service and price. A casino is just up the block and restaurants are also within close walking distance. You can also choose to eat at Victoria Courts own restaurant which serves excellent food.

Ryan, the resident driver even took me around the area for a short tour. Rizal Park, the colonial area and the local fruit markets were some of the places I was able to see during our short trip. I also took the opportunity to feed some of the people who were begging for food that I saw during our ride and later when I walked through the neighborhood. You are likely to see in your travels throughout Manila, women with their children, begging for food and money. Try and take the time to help someone during the course of your trip.

Later that night I visited the casino as a spectator and resisted the temptation to play blackjack. My flight was scheduled for 6:50 am the next morning and I wanted to be there the full three hours prior to that time just to be sure I could check in on time. I left Manila headed back to Atlanta, GA with stops in Nagoya, Japan and Detroit Michigan. Another great journey was under my belt and I looked forward to the next one.

CHAPTER FIFTEEN

Mostly Beauty and Some of the
Beast of Rio de Janeiro, Brazil

Brazil was on my list of "must see" places for a long time and finally getting an opportunity to go was a thrill in itself. Considered by many as the home of some of the most beautiful women in the world, Brazil has even much more to offer.

From the popular attractions such as Sugar Loaf Mountain, the Trijuca Forest, A Day in Rio, the Tropical Island and the Christ The Redeemer Statue to the great beaches of Copacabana and Ipanema, there is so much to keep you busy during your stay. Brazil gets worldwide recognition in the media for producing beautiful women who regularly compete in the Miss Universe competition but there is also much media attention given to another side of Brazil. The favelas have been portrayed as a very dangerous place to go because they are run by gangs but when I visited the Rocinha Favela I saw something different. I saw a bustling community of people working hard with their businesses and conducting themselves in a peaceful manner.

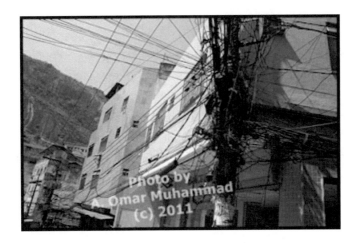

In Rocinha, which is the largest favela in Rio, there are approximately 54,000 houses set in 64,000 meters of space. The majority of houses are made with brick and cement. Most people have electricity and running water but the wiring is sometimes done by someone in the Favela instead of by the government. The meters are sometimes cut off to save the residents money according to my tour guide Patricia Furtado, The cheapest places to live is closer to the top of the hill. The more expensive houses and apartments are at the bottom of the hill. The average price for a two bedroom house is about $30-35,000 reais. At the bottom of the hill is double. Rocinha is a busy place and with only 1 main road, there's a lot to see. There is one entrance and that is also the only exit. That makes it easy to control and secure. You will see boys or men at the entrance with guns but they are not aggressive at all. Furtado said that it is the gangs who keep the peace in the favela and they will not allow drugs like crack cocaine to integrate in because it is so addictive and would destroy the community.

There are many shops, bars and hang out places. People in the streets are friendly and greet each other. We walked around during my tour, ate frozen acai deserts and visited the meat market where they had fresh chickens. At the bottom of the hill, there are street vendors and people hanging out.

There are also schools such as Parati Amizade E Solidariedade, that benefit from the favela tour. RPT Tours can also arrange a favela tour. The tour cost about 60 reais. The government, who currently only controls a small percentage of favelas has now vowed to take them over from the drug dealers because Rio was hosting the 2014 World Cup.

The favela tour is only a half day so I had time that night to go to Barra (pronounced Baha), where the Rock in Rio concert was going on.

Everyone was talking about this event that included many latin entertainers and also featured Rihanna, Stevie Wonder and Shakira. It covered two weekends of shows and the audience numbers are about 700,000. The bus ride from Rio is normally about 45 minutes but with everyone converging in on Barra for Rock in Rio, the ride took about three hours to get there. The droves of people headed to the gate reminded me of the Million Man March. It was crazy! I was burnt out however from the ride over there so I just took a few photos and headed back to Rio to get some rest.

The next day Wakeel and I had to move to a different apartment. We had only booked two days in Copacabana with Rio Rentals 4 Less. John Thompson, a retired New York police officer who has lived in Rio for about 20 years now, was Wakeel's contact person and also acted as our interpreter. He moved us into another two bedroom apartment that was also in Copacabana. He also got another room for Wakeels friend Chaison who had arrived a few days before us. You can reach John in Rio at 9971-8479.

Photo by
A. Omar Muhammad
(c) 2011

The next day was the Tropical Tour which costs 90 reais and included a two and one half hour ride to the marina where we boarded a sailboat and headed out to visit four different islands. There are a total of about 365 Islands in Brazil. If you want a peaceful day out on the water with the chance to take some great photos, then take this tour.

The excursion included one stop designed for snorkeling so I took advange of that for an additional 10 Reais to rent the equipment. It was great to see so many fish crowded around the boat. The last island is where we enjoyed the delicious buffet that included fish, rice, beans, green salad, carrots and cucumber salad. We headed back across the water to the dock to conclude our sailboat tour. The trip was great in spite of terrible traffic we ran into because of the Rock in Rio concert.

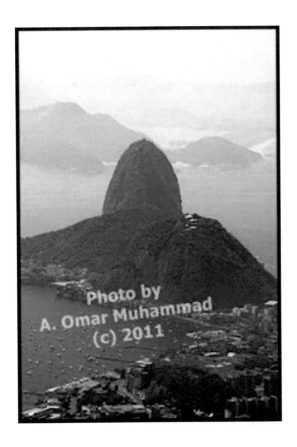

Photo by A. Omar Muhammad (c) 2011

The next day I chose the Day in Rio Tour which is a full day of various locations including the Trijuca Forest, Corcovado Mountain, the Carnival Rehearsal location, and the Cathedral. The tour guide was Ilda Gomes Crespo and can be contacted at 8221-7462. We made stops to take photos at Ipanema beach then had a great lunch buffet at the Grill Inn and for the finale we headed to Sugar Loaf Mountain for a fantastic aerial view.

There you ride on cable cars using lifts to the first mountain top. Then you board another cable car to go even higher up to the next mountain. The views are spectacular from the heights of these mountains, which at the peak is 1,299 feet. It was a full day of touring from 9:00 am to about 5:30 pm. The cost of the tour was 135 reais.

I was scheduled to leave Rio, so I was dropped off at the Rio mall to catch a bus to the airport. The bus cost only 9 reais for the one hour ride whereas a taxi would cost about 40 reais during the day and 60 reais at night. there are different rates and the taxi meter will show whether you are being charged the day rate or night rate which is indicated by a 1 or a 2 on the meter. Since I did not get a seat on the plane due to my standby status, I took the recommendation of the tour guide and went to Lapa for some nightlife. When we arrived there we heard music playing and saw plenty of food vendors cooking hot dogs, burgers and shish-kabobs. The area is blocked off to traffic and the people are dancing in the streets. Musicians were playing music and everyone seemed to be having a good time.

There is also a club called Rio Solarium which is very popular and has three floors of dancing. We let there about 3:00 am and headed for one of the most griddy, grimy and sexually explicit areas known as Villa Mimosa. Some even describe it as "hell on earth". The main focal point of action centers around a building that houses about 40 or 50 different rooms that are equipped with loud music, a bar and women dressed in bikinis or negligee's. Each separate room seems to be competing against the others for the most attention to draw in customers who they can entertain with sexual favors in rooms located above the entry room.

The guys roll in and out of these rooms like there is a sale at the mall, some making deals and some moving on to the next room. Sometimes awful smells exist in the corridors and 90% of the women are not good looking. They range from the young to the old. I saw one that look about 65 and some looked as if they are hooked on drugs. They do not even compare to the prostitutes who hangHAPTER out at a Balcony which is a bar in the Copacabana beach area. The women at the Balcony Bar look and dress very fine and will approach you and ask you to spend about 200 reais with them for one hour.

For some girls, one customer will pay their rent for one week. There are also some men who try to pass as women in both places. Prostitution is legal in Rio but brothels are illegal.

It seems that Brazil has a much different perspective on sexuality than does America. They appear to be free when it comes to there bodies and speaking about sex. Keeping good health and a good looking body seems to be of great value and you will see many natives along with tourists working out along the beachfront areas.

I spent my final day in Rio at the beach relaxing and swimming and later on I walked to the Hippie Fair in Ipanema to buy some t-shirts. We caught a taxi to the airport and this time I got a seat in first class. This was a wonderful experience filled with the beauty, adventures and even some the gritty side of Rio.

Chow!

CHAPTER SIXTEEN

My Journey to South Africa

I left Atlanta, GA in August around 7:30pm and landed at the O.R. TAMBO International Airport in Johannesburg, South Africa around 5:00 pm the next day. It is about a 14 hour flight and they are six hours ahead of Eastern Standard Time in the US.

I was not sure what to expect since I had read and heard so many different things about this part of the world, some negative and some positive. I am glad that I have been afforded the opportunity to visit this continent of Africa even though my original intention was to travel to West Africa, to Ghana or Senegal or other points in West Africa.

I was joined on this trip by Wakeel Allah and his friend Dr Wesley. The first night we found an accommodation called the Mojadji Guest House which is in the Kempton Park area near the airport. It is a bed and breakfast home owned by Dion and Maridi. Dion is now a somewhat liberal Afrikaner after being, as he said, "forced" to join the army at a young age during the period of unrest better known as Apartheid. They have a quaint place that would be more enjoyable in the warmer months between December and March instead of in August, which is winter time in South Africa. They did have a fire burning in the communal area but the rooms were very cold. They did provide portable heaters in our rooms. We only stayed one night as we were ready to venture out the next morning to take in some sights. The owners were both impressed and tickled when I got up and prepared breakfast, including salmon cakes and eggs. They had only prepared oatmeal, or "porage" as it is called there, because we had expressed the night before that we required a pork free meal. The room rate was R250 per person, which is stated as 250 RAND. That is equal to about $40.00 in US money.

They were very hospitable and even took us to a local restaurant after we checked in. That is where we met Jabu, a waiter in Dros Restaurant, who told that his friend Mark could take us on a tour.

Mark took us around to various places and areas of Jo'Burg, as it is called, including the Hillbrow area, the Apartheid Museum, the Mandela House Museum, Sakhumzi Restaurant and various parts of Soweto. We talked to some young vendors who turned out to be aspiring rap artists, who gave us an impromptu performance. We even found Winnie Madikezela Mandela's home but was informed by the security that she was not home.

I would haved loved to sit and speak with her. When she visited Atlanta, GA in 2010, I was blessed to greet her and give her a copy of the DVD of her 1999 visit to the WISOMMM offices run by Fredrica Bey. I also gave her a copy of my book. She gave me the biggest hug and it made me smile from ear to ear. I think she would remember me if she saw me.

After our tour we looked for another guest house and found a very reasonably priced one called the Johannesburg Backpackers located at 14 Umgwezi Road in Emmarentia but it was not easy to find. We got assistance from some Muslim brothers who were outside of the Masjid, who guided us to the location, which turned out to be walking distance to the Masjid.

The room had three bunk beds in a dorm style setting, no television and no heat. I did not complain since the room rate was only R100 for each of us. So that is about $15.00 per night in US money. The shared areas did have a flat screened TV which displayed MTV videos most of the time. They also had a shared kitchen for everyone to use. So we checked in, then went back out to a plaza that had a good amount of eateries and nite-life places and was within walking distance.

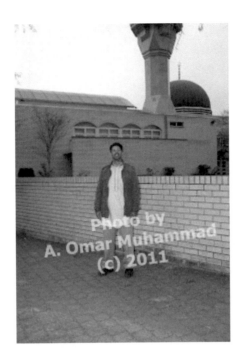

The next day we got a late start but we made it to the Masjid for Jumuah and then had a chance to talk to some of the Muslims and meet Imam Burhaan Mia. All of those I met had a great spirit and freely shared information. Afterward we walked to Cappella's Restaurant and the owner and one of his patrons were gracious enough to allow us to use their internet connectors while we ordered our food. They even prepared a special order of soup with fresh garlic and onion. I was trying to build up my defense mechanism to ward off the germs Wakeel had been spreading with his cold.

The Masjid, The Jo'Burg Guest House and Cappellas are all located in an area called Emmarentia, which is a suburb of Jo'Burg and is not well known even amongst some taxi drivers, but I would urge visitors to go there, even if only for a day.

When we arrived back at the guest house, I played a few games of pool then watched a bit of Soldiers Story on my laptop before turning in. My goal was to get to sleep before Wakeel came back in and started snoring. They had went back out to a town called Rosebank which was not far away.

The next day we got up early and I suggested that we relocate to
another area. This suburb was nice but it did not give you the
authentic feel of Africa, the same as a place like Soweto. So, we
agreed and went and caught a meter taxi to the Jo'Burg bus and
rail station. We began checking prices for buses going to places like
Cape Town, Durban and Pretoria. The Pretoria fare was only R9
which is about $1.25 in US money and the fare to Durban was R135
each way, but in the process of deciding what to do and where to
go, Wakeel and Wesley decided that it was time for them to head
back to Atlanta instead.

I, like the soldier and adventurer that I am, decided to stay in South Africa. I hadn't yet seen enough and had not taken any photos of any animals at this point. I decided to take a meter taxi, which by the way only cost R10 per person for a one way ride to many areas in and around Jo'Burg. When you exit the bus station many vendors, shoppers, movers, shakers and even trouble seekers are milling around in this bustling area. It is not meant for those who are faint of heart. I met some Muslims on one corner and they recommended that I not walk around solo. Hussein Abdullah and Hassan Nyesa showed me where the meter taxi garage was but the driver misunderstood where I wanted to go and I boarded the taxi to Soweto instead.

It turned out great because I was able to connect with some of the people I had met the day before at the Sakhumzi Restaurant.

This time I also met the owner of the restaurant, Mr. Sakhumzi himself. I enjoyed a delicious meal and was provided great service by Leo who is the manager and Nthabeleng, one of the waitresses who also had experience in hosting video productions.

I interviewed the owner, took some photos and headed back to the main road to flag down a meter taxi. To get back to Jo'Burg you need to be on the correct side of the road and raise up one finger which signifies that you are going out of the area you are currently in. The correct taxi somehow knows to stop for you. The payment process is also very interesting. You do not pay when you first get in the taxi but at a certain time the collection begins.

The people begin passing the fare towards the front and the passenger sitting next to the driver is responsible for keeping track of the money and passing back the change. I told some of those riding that that process was amazing and I could not imagine that happening in the U.S.A., without a fight breaking out at certain times.

I made it to the Masjid in Emmarentia for Iftar and prayer and made an appointment to interview Imam Burhaan, so he could talk about the history of Islam in South Africa and in his immediate area. When I got back to the guest house I made arrangements to take a short tour the next day to visit the Lion Park. It was much more than I anticipated.

Not only was I able to pet some of the cubs, one of which tried to bite me after growling, but we also interacted with the giraffe's and drove thru various park sections bringing us up close and personal with huge lions, zebra and antelope. Our driver and guide is known as Captain Morgan, a very charismatic man of 38 years who still has dreams of becoming a professional boxer. We left the Lion Park and stopped at a shopping plaza for a great African meal before heading back.

It was still early so I just walked to the local plaza in Emmarentia to use the internet in the Tokyo Cafe and then headed back in to call it a night. They next day I decided I had seen enough for this visit and made plans to get to the airport. I called Captain Morgan but due to his schedule he could not make it but sent one of his co-workers instead. The driver, Lavette, like Captain Morgan was originally from Zimbabwe. He arrived at about 10:00 am and thought I was ready to go directly to the airport. I explained to him that my flight was not until 8:20pm and I wanted to tour some areas before going to the airport. We negotiated a full day of riding for R1000 which is about $100 in US money.

So our first stop was back to Soweto so I could take a copy of my book "I Met An Angel" to some of those at the Sakhumzi Restaurant. I took a few photos with Leo, the manager. The next stop was the ANC office to attempt to get an interview with Julius Malema, the charismatic leader of the ANC Youth movement. Nthabeleng joined us as a host and would have been able to express my questions in the native language but he was not available and due to my schedule and plans to leave South Africa that night, they only provided an email address to make the appointment. So we dropped Nthabeleng back in Soweto and headed for Sandton, which is a developed area that includes large hotels, malls and even boasts being the home of the huge Mandela statue that stands in the courtyard one of the mall.

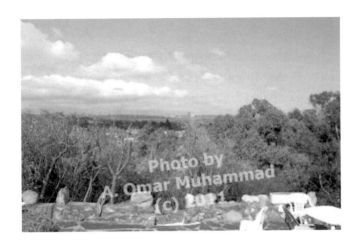

I headed to the airport but unfortunately there were no available seats to fly out, so I went back into my notes to find another guest house that was close to the airport and had a shuttle service for R100. I found the Backpacker's Ritz located at 1A North Road in Dunkeld West which is about a 30 minute ride away. Their shuttle service shuts down by 7:30pm so I still had to hire a taxi which costs R300. The room fee was R125 so, that's about $18.00 in US money, but the taxi ran about $54.00 US.

The guest house was situated about 45 minutes walking distance to the mall and train station. The Rosebank Station also has runs to the airport for R140 and you would just have to transfer in Sandton. That is ideal for backpacker's and those who travel light.

I learned later that there are other guest houses not far from the area on Breely Street close to Alexander Township. It seems that they are not easily found on the internet when doing research. I did get a decent night sleep at the Ritz after watching part of movie in the communal room. It was a bit chilly and musty in the dorm room that had about eight bunk beds that were mostly occupied that night.

The next day I got up and prepared some oatmeal in the communal kitchen. When traveling I believe in bringing food along to help save money by keeping me out of restaurants everytime I get hungry.

I caught the shuttle to the Rosebank Mall and looked around in some of the shops before going to Nino's Restaurant. I ordered the butternut squash soup and it was delicious! I followed it with some mint tea with honey the caught another taxi back to the guest house.

I used the "pay for your use" internet for an hour or so but didn't get much done because of their super slow system. I got the feeling that the system was rigged so you would have to continue buying time. My second trip to the airport was upon me. I was hopeful but I still did not get an assigned seat so I stayed thoughout the night in the airport forming a bed out of my four suitcases. It was the only time I was glad I bought four bags with me. Traveling light is a great option.

South Africa was special and I would visit again with a carefully mapped out itinerary. My suggestions to others are to visit Soweto and Alexander and some southern Jo'Burg areas and find guest houses in those areas that will give you the real feel of Africa or spend a little more and stay in a hotel where you can enjoy privacy, heat, hot water and other amenities. Safety is a real concern in Johannesburg, like most places in the world that you are not familiar with, so travel with others, be cautious, but do enjoy yourself!

Peace and good travels!

CHAPTER SEVENTEEN

How to Travel to Costa Rica on a Budget

As usual, when planning a trip, I go to various websites searching for clues, reviews, discount lodging, activities and money exchange rates. You may want to note that Costa Rica uses colones as the medium of exchange but also accept US dollars in most places. Generally speaking, 1,000 colones are equal to two US dollars, so when calculating colones just move the decimal over (to the left) three places and multiply by two to get the US dollar equivalent.

So with the assistance of my son Omar, who would also be joining me on this trip to Costa Rica, we began our research checking Frommers.com, TripAdvisor.com, Hostels.com, GoVisitCostaRica.com, Google Maps, and other websites to get somewhat familiar with that part of the world.

There were no flights available to the San Jose airport, so we decided to fly Delta to the Liberia Airport (LIR). Liberia is located in the Guanacaste Province which is located in the Northeastern part of Costa Rica. This is not a bad option for anyone who wants to see the country in the most cost effective way, which is by bus. We took a taxi from the airport and checked in the the Boyeros Hotel in downtown Liberia. The taxi charge was $15.00 for me and my son. There is however, an even cheaper way to get to the center of Liberia. You can take a taxi out to the main road for about $4.00 and take the local bus for only 50 cents. That is how we returned to the airport on our departure day.

Photo by A. Omar Muhammad (c) 2011

The Boyeros was a nice hotel with a 24 hour restaurant and two swimming pools (one adult and one child pool with little waterfall). They also had double beds, cable TV and hot water. The staff does not speak much English so brush up on your Spanish before your trip. Many small hotels and hostels do not have hot water so always check your room and turn on the water before payment is given especially if you travel without making advance reservations like we did. They are also conveniently located on the bus line and around the corner from the bus station.

The cost of the room was $60.00 per night, which was over our hotel budget of $40.00 per night, but the hot water and nice pool was a good trade off. We spent the day at the pool, getting adjusted and planning our next move. We did not eat at their restaurant but instead walked across the road to a food mall which housed Burger King and a few other fast food restaurants. It was packed with locals and a few tourists. After eating we stocked up on water and headed back to the hotel. My son Omar crashed out and I stayed up and got treated to a Pacquiao vs. Margarito fight on HBO.

Photo by A. Omar Muhammad (c) 2011

We got up early at about 4:30 AM to make our six and a half hour trip to the Manuel Antonio National Park, which was one of the places that showed up on many websites and was a "must see" type of location. I paid $12.00 for us to go to Barranca, which was about an hour and a half away. For $1.00, we took the local bus to the Puntarenas Bus Station. You must purchase a bus ticket at the booth around the corner from where the buses line up.

The bus to Manuel Antonio cost $15.00 and was another two hour ride. We really were able to take in the beautiful scenery of the country as we rode the highway in this comfortable bus. We arrived about 11:00 AM in Quepos and decided to find a hotel there instead of riding to Manuel Antonio which was only a short 30 minute ride away. We walked about two blocks and found the Park Hotel or Hotel Parque which was situated on the 2nd floor over the Drage Pharmacy. It was very quaint with only cold water and no air conditioning but it did have cable TV and a ceiling fan and only cost $20.00 for the room that we selected with two twin beds. We checked in and dropped our bags and scurried back to the bus station to continue our journey to the Manuel Antonio National Park. There is a $10.00 entry fee for adults and it was free for my son who was 11 years of age. You have to walk about a mile on a gravel and dirt road before reaching the beach. We did not see any wildlife along the way as it was promoted in their literature and on some websites. The walk was a bit grueling in the heat and with our backpacks but the beach was beautiful and the water was fine.

Actually, my recommendation would be to pass on going through the National Park and instead just go on the other side of the road and enjoy the beach right there. There are noticeably more rocks and stones along the shoreline and you can't avoid walking on them as you enter the ocean but the $10.00 National Park fee could then be used for a meal or two. After a while the clouds rolled in and it began to rain. My son was undaunted and continued to swim. After his hands and feet resembled raisins, we headed back up the pathway and decided to eat at Chicken on the Run, which is situated on the main road and right across from the beach, before heading back to the hotel. We shared a whole rotisserie chicken, rice and beans, plantains and a two liter bottle of soda, which cost about $16.00 for everything. Be mindful however, that the chicken and other livestock that you eat are likely raised on the same water that you are trying to avoid when you purchased bottled water during your stay.

Just as you experience illness, cramps and vomiting in Mexico and are warned "don't drink the water", the same warning should also apply when visiting Costa Rica.

We scheduled the Mangrove Safari Tour for the next day then jumped back on the local bus to Quepos for $1.00 and was safely in our room by about 7:00 PM. After our cold showers, Omar watched the Disney Channel in Spanish, while I went to Bogarts Restaurant just downstairs and to the right, to use the internet to plot our next moves.

I checked the bus schedules at www.thebusschedule.com to make sure we stayed on schedule.The next morning we got up early and checked out of the hotel. We carried our bags with us to the tour pick up location in Manuel Antonio because we were going to get a bus to San Jose right after the safari tour. We could have gotten picked up at the hotel but when I signed up for the tour the previous day, I did not know the exact name or location of the hotel, so to avoid confusion, I said we would just come to the ticket booth location. Little did I know that the mini tour bus would end up taking us right back to Quepos to a restaurant less than a half block from the hotel to have lunch, which was included in the $65.00 per head ticket pice of the tour. The food was good and included rice and beans, salad and a choice of fish or chicken. The tour drivers appeared confused and not very organized.

They said it was a four hour tour but ended up being about 2 hours. We finally arrived at Damas Island to board th boat about 2 hours after we were picked up. The river area was desolate to say the least.

We saw monkeys right along the bush area near the dock. We also saw some birds in that immediate area but deeper into the ride we saw less and less. No crocodile as promised upon signing up. We did see a curled up snake that appeared to be sleeping on a tree branch. One lady on the tour, from San Francisco, CA said she had taken the tour about 20 years ago and the same area was filled with colorful birds swooping down and flying around in every direction. The tour guide who looked to be in his twenties, could not offer a reason.

My suggestion is to skip this tour or find a company that offers it for about $40.00. That what is seems to be worth. You can also ride over to Damas and you may just be able to see the monkeys hanging around the dock area. If there is a next time, we would likely opt for a trip to a zoo or a reserve like Africa Mia which is located in the El Salto area of Liberia. You can check their website to reserve space at www.africamia.net. We hustled back from the tour and around 5:00 pm we boarded the bus to San Jose. We got there around 8:30 PM and was fortunate to get assistance from two young ladies who were on the bus who provided some information about the bus station area crime. They translated our selected hostel to the taxi driver, who spoke very little English.

We checked in to Vesuvio for $40.00 for the night. It was a great place to stay with hot water, cable TV, AC and free breakfast.

Eduardo and Mauricio spoke excellent English and were very informative and hospitable. Vesuvio can be contacted by visiting there website at http://www.hotelvesuvio.com/ .

After a quick breafast of toast and fruit we took a super quick 30 minute tour of San Jose downtown district. Our bus to Liberia was at 7:00 AM and arrived in Liberia about 11:00 AM which gave us a three hour cushion before our flight back to the USA. We used the time by heading to the local supermarket to purchase some coffee for gifts.

We boarded the local bus and got off at the entry road to the airport, then took a taxi in to the entrance area. Keep in mind that there is an exit tax charged before you leave, so don't spend every dollar you have in Costa Rica or you may have an extended stay. The fee is about $26.00 per person.

We arrived back in Atlanta after four hours, went through customs and baggage check and finally to our vehicle. My son and I had accomplished a great deal in only four days and three nights. We spent less than $500.00 dollars on ground transportation, food, hotels, gifts and entertainment. When my son looked over to me and said "thank you for taking me to Costa Rica", simple words alone could not express my gratitude to the Creator. My feeling could justifiably be described as "Muy, Muy Bien"!

TO BE CONTINUED WITH THE NEXT ADVENTURE

And Remember... The World is Yours!

Made in the USA
Columbia, SC
06 August 2024